Poor…but Very, Very Rich

Millennial Mind Publishing
An imprint of American Book Publishing
5442 So. 900 East, #146
Salt Lake City, UT 84117-7204
www.american-book.com
Printed in the United States of America on acid-free paper.

Poor...but Very, Very Rich

Designed by Jana Rade, design@american-book.com

Publisher's Note: American Book Publishing relies on the author's integrity of research and attribution; each statement has not been investigated to determine if it has been accurately made. The author and publisher specifically disclaim any responsibility for any liability, loss, or risk, personal or otherwise, which is incurred as a consequence, directly or indirectly, of the use and application of any of the contents of this book. In such situations where medical, legal, or other professional services may apply, please seek the advice of such professionals directly.

ISBN-13: 978-1-58982-849-0
ISBN-10: 1-58982-849-6

Library of Congress Cataloging-in-Publication Data

Lott, Ruth.
 Poor-- but very, very rich : a personal memoir of growing up in southwest Philadelphia during the 1930s and 1940s / by Ruth Lott ; foreword written by Philip Yancey.
    p. cm.
Includes bibliographical references and index.
ISBN-13: 978-1-58982-849-0 (alk. paper)
ISBN-10: 1-58982-849-6 (alk. paper)
1. Lott, Ruth. 2. Philadelphia (Pa.)--Biography. 3. Philadelphia (Pa.)--Social life and customs--20th century. 4. Philadelphia (Pa.)--History--20th century. I. Title.
F158.5.L68 2012
974.8'11043092--dc23
[B]

2011037366

Special Sales: These books are available at special discounts for bulk purchases. Special editions, including personalized covers, excerpts of existing books, and corporate imprints, can be created in large quantities for special needs. For more information e-mail info@american-book.com.

Poor...but Very, Very Rich

A Personal Memoir of Growing up in Southwest Philadelphia During the 1930s and 1940s.

By Ruth Lott

Foreword written by Philip Yancey

Dedication

This memoir is dedicated to my wonderful grandchildren, Andrew and Kristy, who have brought me great joy; to their spouses Brandt and Jessica, who, with her dazzling eyes and infectious laughter, today dances with the angels in the beautiful "Garden of Somewhere"; and in loving memory of my parents; and also my brothers: Jim, Walt, and Bob.

Table of Contents

Foreword

Since Ruth Lott is my mother's sister, and therefore my aunt, I have a built-in interest in this reminiscence. Yet I believe it to be a valuable document for anyone curious about life in the United States in the middle part of the last century. Television journalist Tom Brokaw coined the term "The Greatest Generation" to describe those who grew up in the shadow of the Great Depression and World War II, and those of us born later have much to learn from survivors of this remarkable era.

Imagine life before iPhones and flat-screen televisions, before the Internet and jet planes. Imagine milk and bread delivered to your house on horse-drawn wagons, and mail delivery (including 1-cent post cards) twice a day even on Saturdays. Imagine an urban neighborhood so safe that children walked to school and played on gas-lit streets at night. Imagine an era when nearly everyone went to church on Sunday and 95 percent of babies were born to married couples. Ruth Lott recreates this setting with a sharp eye for detail.

For me, this memoir is a trip back in time, to my childhood, and also further back, to a world hardly recognizable from the one we live in. My grandmother, who presided over the world described here, lived in three centuries: born in 1898, she died in 2000. I'll never forget visiting her after a trip to the crumbling Soviet Union in 1991. I described the momentous changes that I had observed as power was passing from Mikhail Gorbachev to Boris Yeltsin and our long-time enemy Russia was edging toward democracy. "I remember when those boys took over," Grandmother said after hearing my stories; she was referring to the Bolsheviks of 1917. "I didn't think they would last." She, a teenager at the time of the Russian Revolution, went on to outlive Soviet Communism by a full decade.

We review the past not simply to marvel at it but to learn from it, and indeed the Greatest Generation has much to teach us. We moderns have lived through recessions, but nothing like the Great Depression when one-fourth of American workers lost their jobs and Gross National Product fell by almost a third. We have lived through wars, but nothing like World War II, when 417,000 U.S. soldiers died. Somehow, the country survived. More, it emerged stronger than ever, as the dominant nation in the world. In between the lines of *Poor...but Very, Very Rich* you will find clues to that success: a can-do spirit, community support, and neighbors who cared, all fueled by a religious faith based on the Golden Rule.

William Faulkner's lines from his Nobel Prize acceptance speech come to mind: "I believe that man will not merely endure: he will prevail. He is immortal, not because he alone among creatures has an inexhaustible voice, but because he has a soul, a spirit capable of compassion and sacrifice and endurance." We need such reminders, such clarion calls of hope, in times of crisis. Thank you, Aunt Ruth, for reminding us of what we men and women pulling together can do.

Philip Yancey
World renowned award winning author and speaker; editor at large of *Christianity Today*.

Prologue

These memories of life in Southwest Philadelphia during the 1930s and 1940s are being recorded for two specific reasons.

First, this is written for my son, daughter-in law and grandchildren, and in response to requests from children of cousins for information regarding grandparents, aunts, uncles and cousins, about whom they have heard but never had the opportunity to meet.

In reflecting upon and recording this information, it occurred to me that our own children, grandchildren, and future generations could neither enjoy nor appreciate these experiences without a glimpse into the lifestyle in which they took place. Conditions were so totally different during this period than what they have lived and known. We are products of our environment, circumstances, and experiences, and I firmly believe they contribute to helping to mold our character—and who we become.

Second, recent reports of violence and murders taking place in the area in which we were raised, and about which I have so many wonderful memories, are so disheartening, I want to share with readers another side of life in Southwest Philadelphia as my family knew it and lived it.

These events took place in the 1930s and 1940s--known as the Depression, pre-War, World War II, and post-War eras.

Many changes took place during this time and it was an interesting and challenging period for those of us fortunate to have been a part of it. Hopefully, for some readers, it will be a wonderful trip down "memory lane" as well.

This record includes my memories and vignettes of family life in general. During this period, our lives were significantly influenced by the churches and houses of worship, family, schools, neighbors, friends, and places of employment, as they were at the core of our existence. Money was scarce and people cared about others and banded together to help each other. The "golden rule," as recorded in the Gospels of Matthew 7:12 and Luke 6:31, was taught and practiced.

When work was scarce, employees willingly worked shorter workweeks to give other employees an opportunity to earn some pay that they could take home--which at times was as little as $10/week--to help cover the basic needs of their families.

If someone was ill or died, neighbors always pitched in and provided help where needed. Two or three families often shared a house and expenses to reduce the cost of living.

Materialism, as we know it today, did not exist in our neighborhood. We shared similar circumstances, learned to care about others, and were happy to share their successes with them as well.

Through it all, we survived, and, as a result, we knew happiness during a very difficult period. Yes, we were **"Poor...but Very, Very Rich!"**

Part I
A General Overview

Have you ever wondered what life was like when your parents and grandparents were growing up?

My mother, a descendant of the Penn family, was born in 1898. That was before the days of indoor plumbing, electricity, automobiles, etc. She died in 2000, just shy of the anniversary of her 102nd birthday. During the three centuries in which she lived, this country experienced many changes, providing mother with many wonderful stories to tell.

Often she began conversations with the phrase: "When I was growing up....." and we knew she was about to share some interesting and valuable stories with us about her past, her family, and some of the exciting things she had seen and experienced. How I long to hear them again! Being older and wiser, there are many questions I would ask, and I know I would listen more attentively.

These were enjoyable and valuable experiences for us to learn about as they gave us insight into the past, and helped us to gain an understanding of, as well as an appreciation for, people, places, customs, and things.

During the 1930s and 1940s many changes occurred in Southwest Philadelphia where my family and I lived. Our lifestyle changed as the result of these events and circumstances.

Reflecting on this period has given me the desire to share my treasury of memories with others, as it was a challenging and enriching time. Please accept my invitation to read on and share with me as I recall memories from this wonderful era.

Chapter 1
Overview of Neighborhood and Lifestyle

Born the fifth child of six, life for me began in a twin house in Llanerch Hills, Delaware County, Pennsylvania. (Most births took place at home in those days.) At that time, Llanerch Hills consisted of three streets—Harding, Wilson, and Roosevelt—and a country club.

For those of you who are unfamiliar with the terminology: a twin house is one of two identical houses, built side by side, with adjoining walls but with reverse floor plans. Today they may be called duplexes.

The country was in the throes of a depression, and it became necessary for my family, like others, to move to Southwest Philadelphia to be close to my father's place of employment.

Most of the homes in Southwest Philadelphia were small, two-story row houses with three bedrooms, one bath, and a basement, which was often referred to as a "cellar." Houses like this today are called town homes. They rented for $20-$25/month. If a family found a house that rented for less than they were paying, they often moved out of one house in the middle of the night and into the other house. It was not unusual for people to move just across the street, down the street, over to the next street, or even a block or two away.

My parents bought their house in 1940 with a $100 down payment. Mother saved this amount by putting money away each week into a Christmas club at a local bank. The house cost $2,100 and the monthly mortgage payment was $15, for a period of fifteen years. This house remained in the family and was sold in June 2008, following the death of my brother, Jim, who lived in that house for over 67 years.

The houses were built on narrow streets—thirty to a row. On some streets, the rows of houses were separated by small parks. Often, those who lived in the corner houses ran a small business from an area on the ground and basement levels of their home. Bakeries, drugstores, barber shops, beauty salons, florist shops, real estate offices, medical offices, mom-and-pop grocery stores, tailors, dry cleaners, and shoe repair shops were some of the businesses that found their place among the rows of homes.

Some homes had small backyards with an alley separating them from the backyards of the houses on the next street. Other homes had large backyards extending to an alley beyond which was either a stone wall or a grassy slope leading down to the driveway at the rear of the homes on the neighboring street. There was a grassy slope behind our house which was ideal for sledding and skiing; and filled many hours with fun for us. All yards were separated with hairpin fences made of wrought iron.

Hucksters, shoeshine boys, ragmen, and garbage collectors all used the alleys to conduct business. Ragmen, carrying large burlap bags over their shoulder, collected items such as rags, papers, and any items the people wanted to discard. They carried small spring scales to weigh the items and gave the people a small amount of money in exchange for what they received. They used to walk up and down the alleys saying: "Oh, mamas! Oh, papas! Got any rags today?" (Because of their dialect, we, as kids thought they were calling for and collecting old mommas, old papas, and old people.)

Life was simple in those days and filled with tradition. More attention was spent on the family, rather than on employment and how much money and material items could be gained. People cared for and about each other.

Automobiles were few and far between so traffic problems were relatively nonexistent. Because of this and the fact that illegal drug usage and violence were not prevalent in those days, the streets were safe and we children were able to roam throughout the neighborhood without fear either on our part or that of our parents. Generally, parents did not have to set parameters beyond which their children were not permitted to go.

Groups of children were often seen playing various games together in the street throughout most of the days and evenings when they were not in school or participating in other activities. It was a happy experience for the children, and parents watched out for their children as well as for the children of their friends and neighbors. Laughter filled the air as we raced up, down, and across the street during our play. They were indeed carefree days.

We were taught manners and respect for one another and for the belongings of others. We were taught and expected to live by the "golden rule." School days always began with the salute to the flag, the reading of ten verses of scripture from the Bible, and a silent prayer, and it was customary to begin each meal with a prayer of thanks, also known as "grace." Bedtime prayers were always said at the end of the day.

The Golden Rule
"So in everything, do to others as you would have them do to you, for this sums up the Law and the Prophets."
    Matthew 7:12

"Do to others as you would have them do to you."
    Luke 6:31[1]

---

[1] Scripture taken from the *Holy Bible, New International Version.* © 1973, 1978, 1984 International Bible Society. Used with permission Zondervan Bible Publishers.

Chapter 2
Churches

Churches of all denominations and other houses of worship were prevalent throughout the area. They provided a wide variety of services and activities for the entire family; and families attended services, together, on a regular basis.

For a period of time, there was also a group known as the "Federation of Southwest Philadelphia Churches" which met on a monthly basis. Representatives from churches of all denominations and races were included, and we had some wonderful times getting acquainted with the people and learning about their beliefs, cultures, and traditions. We had hymn sings, guest speakers, and social gatherings with refreshments. It was a very beneficial and enjoyable experience for all who attended.

Our family attended Southwestern Presbyterian Church at 70th Street and Buist Avenue, which had very active programs for families. There were Sunday school classes for all ages, Sunday morning worship, junior and senior high Christian Endeavor, children as well as junior and senior high choirs, Sunday evening worship including hymn sings, movies, and refreshments, Wednesday evening prayer meeting, Boy, Girl and Cub Scout troops, basketball team, bowling team, etc. These activities provided many learning experiences for us both as individuals and in groups.

Each summer we attended Vacation Bible School (VBS) which was a fun experience. We learned Bible stories about Joseph and his coat of many colors, Baby Moses being placed in a basket in the bulrushes by his sister to save him from being killed by Pharaoh, Jonah and the whale, Daniel in the lion's den, stories of Jesus walking on water, miracles performed by Jesus, etc. These stories were depicted with figures on a flannel graph board. The colorful backgrounds and figures brought the stories to life, and we always had

related crafts to work on and story papers to take home. In addition to the arts and crafts, we sang songs, played games, participated in various sports, and enjoyed refreshments of either juice or milk and graham crackers.

Our pastor, Rev. David H. Curry, was a very loving and compassionate man who was loved by all. He was considered by all to be the "community pastor," and he was invited to participate in many school and community events, including officiating at the funeral of Magistrate Reddy Bell, who was of a different faith.

Pastor Curry, as he was affectionately called, practiced his faith diligently. If he was riding on a trolley car on a Saturday night and the time was approaching midnight, he would get off and walk home because he believed in living by the Ten Commandments. One of the commandments is to, "Remember the Sabbath Day to keep it holy." Pastor Curry believed that by riding on the trolley past midnight he was causing someone to work on the Sabbath day, thus breaking a commandment. He could not and would not do that. He led his congregation by example.

At Vacation Bible School, frequently referred to as VBS, he taught us to play softball and basketball, even though he was quite elderly. He died just four months shy of the 100th anniversary of his birth. I was fortunate to be one of a group of youngsters he took to watch a major league baseball game at Shibe Park. I don't remember if it was the Philadelphia A's or the Phillies who played that day as both clubs shared the park, and I had the privilege of seeing both teams play.

Pastor Curry, together with Charlie's brother who was also a minister, officiated at our wedding and also baptized our infant son.

In my teens, I belonged to a Sunday school class which stayed together throughout high school. We had monthly class meetings (social gatherings) for a number of years and have forged many memories, which keep us laughing even now when we get together and reminisce. Every fall we elected officers, and they each had specific duties to fulfill.

Our class meetings always began with the reading of a passage of scripture, a prayer, the reading of the minutes from the previous meeting, and the report by the treasurer. Many times we had "sentence prayers" and at times it was a competition to see who could offer the longest prayer. The meeting was followed by refreshments. It was not planned but it seemed as though at every gathering someone would ask for a glass of water. The hostess would bring the requested glass of water and, before retaking her seat, would graciously ask if anyone else would like a glass of water. Usually there was no response. It never failed! As soon as the hostess would sit down, someone else would ask for a glass of water. This was repeated a number of times until the hostesses got smart and provided glasses of water for everyone at the beginning of the refreshment period. Most of our conversations usually revolved around boys, which was as common for teenagers then as it is now.

After we married, several of us who lived in nearby towns continued our friendships, and we got together for family picnics, luncheons, and birthday parties with our children. When the children were old enough to enroll in school, we had to make a change, as the new schedules created conflicts.

When that occurred, we decided to hold our get-togethers in the evenings, after the children were settled into bed for the night. The dads were available and willing to babysit for us giving us a "girl's night out". This also gave us quality time to spend together as adults and this practice continued until circumstances took our lives to different areas of the country.

Contact with some of these friends still continues, and several of us also communicate with the daughter of our beloved Sunday school teacher, Grace Hess, who always referred to us as her "girls." Her memory remains very dear to us all, and the lessons she taught us have greatly influenced, enriched, and guided our lives. She was named appropriately because she truly exemplified the epitome of grace in every way.

There are several specific memories which have remained with me over the years that I would like to share with you.

Most of our holiday gatherings were usually hosted at Grace's lovely home. She had a beautiful collection of bone china tea cups and saucers, which her daughter, Naoma, treasures today. We were thrilled and felt so privileged when she served hot tea or hot chocolate in them. It made us feel very grown-up and special, and it helped us to gain an appreciation for the finer things of life. She usually served special food items related to the particular holiday, such as on St. Patrick's Day when she served frog-shaped cupcakes.

Each Christmas, Grace gave each of us a lovely gift. One year she gave us beautifully wrapped packages. We all excitedly opened them with the exception of one of our classmates. She stated she was going to take her gift home and place it under the tree, and open it on Christmas Eve when she and her family gathered to share the tradition together. Curiosity finally got the best of her, and she gave in and opened the package. To her surprise, and to Grace's embarrassment, the box was empty. Grace quickly and graciously remedied the situation. When she wrapped the packages, she had noticed there was an extra box but did not think anything of it and did not bother to look inside. The memory of that empty box has lingered through the years and has provided us with many chuckles.

Another very important lesson we learned from Grace concerned the importance of tithing to the church. One Sunday she related to us that she had put her last dollar in the offering plate, and had just enough tokens to get her to and from work the next day. When she put on her coat the next morning, she put her hand in her pocket, and, to her surprise, she found a $20 bill that she did not know she had. The Christian Faith teaches the concept that everything we have comes from God, the Provider, and we as individuals have the responsibility of giving the first 10 percent of whatever we have to God's work. Everything given over the 10 percent is considered a gift. If we give faithfully, He will provide for all of our needs.

One Sunday a month our class, with the permission of the elders, held a hymn sing, which we called a "singspiration." This was followed by a social gathering where we served refreshments which we bought and paid for with our own money. That activity made us feel grown-up and important. All went well until one evening we served ice cream and pretzels. Some of the older women in the congregation accused us of buying the refreshments on Sunday. That was definitely a "no, no" to that congregation, and also in violation of the Pennsylvania blue laws. The truth is that Grace's brother owned and operated a grocery store. Grace had arranged to purchase the items beforehand, and my father picked them up and delivered them to the church for us. The complaints of these women required us to give an explanation to questions raised by the church elders. There were no laws violated nor were any church teachings compromised.

Every fall the Sunday school observed "rally day" to kick off the beginning of new fall activities following the summer vacation period. During this ceremony, Bibles were presented to the children who were promoted from second grade to third grade in recognition of their promotion from the primary department to the junior department.

In addition, recognition was given for perfect attendance. A pin was given for the first year, a gold wreath to encircle it was given for the second year, and various colored bars signifying additional years were presented for each year the individual attended. (I still have mine.) During the war years, metal was very scarce and the bars had to be exchanged to receive the next one.

Later our family became members of Clearview Methodist Church at 76th Street and Buist Avenue. A long-time beloved family friend, Dr. Thomas A. Buttimer, was appointed to serve as their pastor. As children we attended both churches. We attended Sunday school at Southwestern and then went to worship service with our parents at Clearview.

We also belonged to a weekly Bible club, which met in a private home. This club was part of the Philadelphia Bible Club Movement, which owned and operated Camp Sankanac. Camp Sankanac was located in Pughtown, on the French Creek. It is a beautiful area located outside of Philadelphia.

Participation in the Bible club offered us a time of learning different Bible stories, game playing, and social interaction. Refreshments were always served, and individual birthday anniversaries celebrated with special treats for the honoree. The club met at the home of Mrs. Maxwell, the leader. She had a son, Richard who was in a wheelchair as the result of having had polio, and two daughters: Elsie and Francis Carol. Richard died when he was about 12 or 13 years of age. We eagerly looked forward to attending the club and spending time with this family each week.

Each spring, the Salvation Army (a nondenominational group) assembled and, with a band, marched up and down the streets in full uniform and sang hymns. People gave them monetary donations in response to help their cause as, just like today, they provided for the needy in those days, too.

During the early to mid-1940s, my oldest sister was secretary to the minister of the Philadelphia Gospel Tabernacle, which was located at Broad and Master Streets. That was one of the churches in Philadelphia and other areas that held Youth For Christ (YFC) rallies on Saturday evenings. This provided an inspirational fellowship for them with other young people. Many service personnel also attended and received very warm welcomes. Some of the church members took them to their homes to get acquainted and to provide home-cooked meals and an opportunity to share in some family experiences. The meetings consisted of gospel music with lots of singing and a message brought by a guest speaker. One inspiring and exciting speaker was a country preacher from North Carolina—the well-known and much beloved Rev. Billy Graham. He truly electrified the audience with his simplistic message taken directly from the Bible—the Word of God.

Other famous religious leaders in that day were the Rev. Percy Crawford, who with his wife, Ruth, had morning radio broadcasts and they operated a Christian bookstore in downtown Philadelphia. They also operated King's College, in New Castle, Delaware and camps for various age groups called Shadowbrook, Mountainbrook and Pinebrook. The Rev. Robert Frazier and his wife, Ella, also had a Christian bookstore in downtown Philadelphia, and conducted daily radio broadcasts. He was known as "the blind evangelist." The Rev. George Palmer also did a daily radio broadcast. The Rev. Jack Wyrtzen broadcasted the *Word of Life* program on a weekly basis from Saranac Lake, New York; and Dr. Fuller's *Old Time Gospel Hour*, could also be heard on Sundays. The services on the radio provided comfort and a means of worship for shut-ins and others who were unable to get out and participate in a formal worship service at one of the local churches.

Chapter 3
Communication

Most communication at that time was done by personal visitation. Other methods included:

Mail - Handwritten notes, cards, and letters were the most popular method of communication and very welcome. Children were encouraged to communicate with friends and relatives in that socially acceptable and proper way. Post cards cost one cent to mail and were referred to as the "penny post card."

Letters and cards sent in an envelope cost two cents each to mail. It was a common practice to send picture post cards to friends and family when one was vacationing. Many people collected these and pasted them into albums. They made a nice keepsake which, when passed down through the family, can still be enjoyed today.

Mail delivery to the front door was twice a day, six days a week, except for the pre-Christmas period. At that special time, mail was also delivered on Sundays and as often as three or four times a day. Waiting for the mailman to come was an exciting pastime. Children particularly eagerly awaited the arrival of items ordered from coupons in cereal boxes. They also ordered the Captain Midnight decoder ring and/or Jack Armstrong decoder badge which were featured on the daily radio programs to drinkers of the popular Ovaltine, or whatever product was being promoted by their sponsor.

Newspapers were delivered to the home by paperboys, and were also available at corner newsstands, as well as at local general and drugstores. During World War II, extra copies were printed and distributed. Newsboys walked up and down the streets or stood on corners yelling, "Extra! Extra! Read all about it!"

There were three major papers in the city at that time: The Philadelphia Inquirer was published in the morning but during the war it also published an issue late in the evening. The Philadelphia Evening Bulletin was the late afternoon or evening paper. The Daily News, a smaller paper, was available throughout the day.

Paperboys, usually teenagers, had specified routes and they delivered papers daily after school, via wagon or bike, directly to the front doorstep. Yes, at times they missed while showing off their throwing skills and the paper landed on the rooftop. It was also their responsibility to collect the money owed for the weekly deliveries on Friday afternoons.

Radio broadcasting was a very popular link between the home and the outside world. We had one large, tube set--a Philco--in our home until I was sixteen. As a birthday gift, I received a small white table radio. The *950 Club* was very popular among teens. That program broadcasted wonderful music, and listening to it was an enjoyable pastime. Some of the other programs we listened to on radio included: soap operas, *The Lone Ranger, Jack Armstrong, Captain Midnight, Fibber McGee and Molly, George Burns and Gracie Allen, Queen for* *a Day, the Great Gildersleeve,* and the nightly news. *Gabriel Heatter* was the program most adults listened to at the end of the day to get an update on the latest news, particularly during the war. The program always closed with a rendition of "When the blue of the night meets the gold of the day, someone waits for you," which was sung by a female singer. *Dawn Patrol* broadcasted all the latest hits during the wee hours of the morning, which was especially appreciated by those working the "graveyard shift."

Telegrams (also known as Western Union "wires") were used mostly for emergency notifications. The charge was fifty cents per word, and the word "STOP" was used to separate phrases and to reduce the length and cost of the message. Telegrams usually indicated "trouble."

Telephones were scarce and very few homes had them until the late 1940s. It was necessary to go to the local drug store and use the pay phone if calls had to be made. This was a great inconvenience and offered no privacy. Calls within the city from the payphone cost five cents for three minutes. Many people had to place their names on a waiting list, and when they did get phone service, they often had to share it with a two or three-party line. The number of calls that could be made in a month was limited. The first phone I remember seeing was a stand-up French phone with a round dial. (Cell phones weren't even on the drawing board at that time---and can you believe we survived?) The first phone our family had was installed when I was about sixteen. We were limited to about thirty to forty-five calls per month within the city. Calls outside the city cost ten cents for a limited time, probably three minutes. We considered ourselves to be very fortunate because we did have a single-party line, and it became a very important and popular convenience for everyone.

Television was in its infancy in the late 1940s. Our first set was a gift at Christmas 1950. It was black and white and had a small twelve-inch screen. Color TV was not yet available on the market for home usage.

Television brought great entertainment into our homes. The channels were limited to three major ones (Cable was not yet available to the general public!), but we had a good assortment of programs to watch including: sports, news, *I Love Lucy, Milton Berle, Jackie Gleason, Bob Hope, Perry Como, Dinah Shore, Art Linkletter's House Party* and game shows which were later followed by the daytime soap operas.

Also in the late 1940s, a new show emerged and was called the *American Bandstand*. It was hosted by Bob Horn and later followed by the ever loving and very popular Dick Clark. It was without a doubt the most popular show for young people. Many teenagers gathered at the studio daily after school to participate in the program. Others rushed home from classes so they wouldn't miss one minute of their favorite program. Teenagers identified with the "regulars" who attended the show and thoroughly enjoyed watching the show which kept them abreast of the many songs and dances as they became popular hits.

Chapter 4
General Activities

As I stated previously, life was simple in those days and revolved around the family, the home, the churches and places of worship, the schools, and places of employment. TV was not available in the homes until the mid to late 1940s, but there were many activities that kept us occupied and we were quite busy and content.

Movie Theatres - There were five movie theatres in our immediate neighborhood--the Lindy, the Benn, the Benson, the Orient, and, after World War II, the Airport. Saturday matinees cost ten cents and attendees could stay all afternoon. In addition to the feature film, they showed cartoons and news briefs. Guests at birthday parties were frequently treated to an afternoon at the movies after gathering at the home of the birthday child for cake, ice cream, and the opening of gifts. It took the place of playing games, and the children loved the chance to go to the movie theatre. Moms liked it too, because it meant less mess to clean up and the noise made by the excited children was diverted elsewhere.

As a promotion aimed at increasing attendance at the theatres, many theatres gave away dishes. One night a week was set aside and women interested in collecting a set of dishes frequented the movies and encouraged friends and relatives to go with them to help them collect the desired dishes. In addition to collecting the dishes and the entertainment the movie provided, it also gave them a night out and something to which they could look forward each week.

Indoor Activities - Indoor games included: checkers, jacks, old maid, pig, fish, anagrams, bingo, lotto, pit, paper dolls, button, button, who's got the button?, tiddlywinks, spin the bottle, pin the tail on the donkey, coloring books, and scrapbooks. Playing with dolls and accessories was also a popular and fun activity which the girls enjoyed, as well as pickup sticks.

Scrapbooking was a family affair. Unlike scrapbooking of today, each child had his/her own scrapbook and it was a family affair. All members of the family sat around the table going through magazines. Each child took turns selecting which picture or pictures they wanted to have cut out and pasted into their individual scrapbook. Paste was made by mixing flour and water.

When Monopoly was introduced, it was cost prohibitive for most families. Many of the older youngsters made their own game and gathered on various porches and enjoyed playing it by the hour.

Outdoor Activities - Since the houses were small—and by today's standards they were indeed very small—children were encouraged to spend a great deal of time outdoors.

There was an abundance of children in the area so we never had a shortage of playmates. Some of the outdoor games we enjoyed included: hopscotch, jumping rope, half ball, hose ball, dodge ball, roller skating, croquet, hide and seek, red rover, kite flying, mother, may I, and sledding in the winter. (Note: half balls were made from cutting hollow balls in half, and hose balls were made by cutting rubber hoses into pieces about four inches long, and then hitting them with an old broomstick.) Football and softball were confined to being played in the "fields" or at the schoolyard.

Picnics - Picnics were popular family outings during this period of time. One year dad's employer arranged for train transportation and hosted a day at the New Jersey shore for all employees and their families. What an experience that was! A train ride, a trip to the shore, and a picnic all in one day! What more could anyone—young and old alike---ask for?

Many churches had annual picnics and encouraged participation by all family members. They had games, races,

and peanut scrambles for different age groups. One place our church held their picnics was Bartram's Garden. It was the homestead of the famous botanist, John Bartram, and was situated on the Schuylkill River. A tour of the home took us back in history. I particularly recall the sandy bed at the edge of the river. Someone started a story that it was "quicksand" and would swallow us up if we stepped on it. Of course, we were afraid to go too close to the river. Obviously that was the purpose behind telling the story. The riverbank was covered with a black substance, probably oil from the ships.

Among other things, we were also impressed by the cider press where apples were processed to make apple cider, and, unbelievably, there was an outdoor concrete bathtub.

These outings were cancelled when the war broke out due to lack of transportation, gas rationing, and overall safety. (Note: After the war, picnics resumed and our church picnics were held at the grounds surrounding a church in Secane, (which later became a large home development) Lenape Park, Forest Park, Willow Grove, Woodside and other amusement parks which we enjoyed more as we were older.)

Swimming - There were two local swimming pools--one on Elmwood Avenue and one on Woodland Avenue, both of which were in walking distance from our home. A neighbor also introduced us to swimming at League Island Park, which was closed to the public and became off limits when World War II began because of its close proximity to the naval shipyard.

Skating and Biking - We roller-skated on sidewalks and rode tricycles (bikes for those lucky enough to have one) and scooters. The boys made scooters out of orange crates and roller skates which were fun to ride, when they were willing to share. After putting the time and energy into making a scooter, the boys felt a great sense of pride. They often worked together to help each other build them, but they didn't want the girls to share them. That was considered a boy's activity in those days, and girls weren't supposed to ride them.

Chapter 5
Holiday Observance Traditions

Philadelphia was a melting pot of people from many ethnic backgrounds, and, with the area being steeped in tradition, it was customary to take advantage of the many widespread celebrations of the various holidays. This gave us a greater knowledge and understanding of, as well as an appreciation for, others and their cultures.

There was also a great interaction between the churches, the home, and the schools, and we were privileged to participate in the enriching, multiple holiday celebrations.

New Year's Eve. Our parents always awakened us a few minutes before midnight so we could join in the neighborhood celebration. Some years, depending on finances, we had party hats and horns; other years we just banged pots, pans, and lids together to welcome in the new year. Neighbors ran up and down the street greeting one another and wishing them well for the coming year.

New Year's Day. We were always thrilled by the annual Mummers' Parade. Members of various string bands dressed in brilliantly colored, sequined, and feathered costumes and marched up Broad Street to city hall in center city. The theme song was "O, dem Golden Slippers". They were also accompanied by the comic units. The tradition continues to this day and is a sight to behold. Friends of our family lived at Broad and Ritner Streets, and some years we had front row seats to watch the parade in a warm environment. We greatly appreciated this invitation, since January 1st is usually very cold in Philadelphia, and not conducive to lengthy outdoor stays. Their mother also prepared a large pot of soup, and hot dogs and sauerkraut, which is a tradition in Philadelphia for New Year's Day, to feed the many guests who had gathered.

Valentine's Day was always celebrated in school with a mailbox made from a decorated carton and into which we placed valentines for our classmates. Someone was usually selected to be the postman and deliver them to the students in the class. We made valentines using lace doilies and red construction paper for our parents. We also exchanged valentines with our friends, relatives, and siblings. Dad always bought mother a large heart-shaped box of chocolates.

Lincoln's and Washington's birthdays were usually separate days off from school, (February 12th and 22nd respectively), to celebrate the lives and contributions of these two great presidents of our country. There was always a play in a special assembly honoring them and other notable citizens born in February prior to the holidays.

Saint Patrick's Day was a day on which everyone wore green, whether or not they were truly Irish, or of Irish descent. In school, we sang Irish songs and made shamrocks out of green construction paper, and watched a drama honoring Irish people. The lively music and dances were very uplifting and were enjoyed by all.

Spring was always welcomed in the schools in various ways. We were taught and sang special spring songs, like "Welcome Sweet Springtime," and did arts and crafts projects relating to it. I remember one teacher reading stories to us titled "Spring is Just Around the Corner", and "Casey at the Bat", both of which were favorites.

Also, we planted lima beans, or some kind of flower seeds, in little paper cups and/or egg shells, and it was fun to watch the plants begin to sprout. We later took them home to be planted.

Easter coincided with spring vacation. Prior to leaving for spring vacation, we made little baskets out of various colored sheets of construction paper. The teachers usually filled them with colored grass, and the day prior to spring vacation, when we went home for lunch, we were told the Easter Bunny came and filled them with jelly beans for us.

Easter was always an exciting day in our house. Every member of the family, when we could afford it, had new clothes to wear to Sunday school and church. Mother often made dresses for the girls. In addition, each one received an Easter basket filled with all kinds of candies. We each always found a milk chocolate hollow egg filled with Hershey Kisses, marshmallow chicks, a chocolate bunny; and, of course, the traditional jelly beans and chocolate-coated coconut cream eggs. All of the baskets had identical contents, even down to the number of jelly beans.

Mother's Day was always celebrated the second Sunday in May. It was traditional for everyone to wear a carnation to honor their mother---white for the deceased and either red or pink if the mother was living. Some years we had real flowers, and other years we wore artificial ones made of crepe paper or similar material. The women in the church dressed in white and conducted the worship services. They ushered, read the scripture, led the prayers, and also delivered the message of the morning. These roles were traditionally filled by men, but they welcomed permitting the women taking over on their special day. After all, it was only one Sunday out of the year.

Mothers were also showered with cards and gifts from their loving children. Some were made in school. The teachers were caring and wanted to be certain every mother was honored in some way, and that the children understood the purpose and true meaning of the day.

Memorial Day was known as Decoration Day and was celebrated early, with children bringing flags to school to be placed on the graves of fallen military personnel by veterans from the American Legion. That was celebrated on May 30th and was an official school holiday. Families generally observed the day with picnics and visits to local cemeteries.

Since it was considered the official "opening of summer" at the seashore, it meant the arrival of summer to the kids. It was customary for mother to remove the clothes from the cedar chest that had been carefully packed away at the end of the previous summer. The clothes were then tried on to see which outfit fit which child, and then they were readied for wear---washed, starched, ironed, altered, etc.

Flag Day, June 14, was also celebrated with a parade, flags, and the singing of patriotic songs. Students dressed in red, white, and blue outfits for the special occasion.

Children's Day was celebrated in the churches on the second Sunday in June. Children memorized special songs and recitations which they performed for the adults. Since this occurred after Memorial Day, it was permissible to wear white clothing and white shoes. Traditionally, with the exception of women on Mother's Day, wearing white was only an acceptable custom between Memorial Day and Labor Day.

Father's Day was celebrated in the churches on the third Sunday in June. Aside from that, it was a day for private group celebrations by each family. Many had picnics and honored dads with gifts and cards. It was customary for men to wear hats in those days---felt in the winter and straw, known as '*Panamas*' in the summer.

Gift certificates for hats and shoes were a popular gift for dads. They were placed in a gift box along with a miniature plastic hat or shoe, and were always welcomed as a gift by dads, along with the usual gifts of socks, shirts and ties.

Fourth of July was always an important day in Philadelphia, considered to be the birthplace of our nation, and each community had its own method of celebrating. Southwest Philadelphia was no different. Committee members collected fifty cents from each household in the area bounded from 64th Street to 70th Street, and Elmwood Avenue to Dorel Street. Beyond Dorel Street, there were acres and acres of vacant land, commonly referred to by the kids as "the fields."

Each child in every household received a ball, a flag, and a Japanese straw hat. All the children decorated their trikes and bikes with red, white, and blue paper streamers. There was always a large parade throughout the neighborhood and prizes were given for the best decorated bike or trike.

Following the parade, everyone gathered at the fields for a large picnic. Games and races were held and free hot dogs, chips, pretzels, soda, and ice cream in little Dixie cups were available for everyone who attended throughout the day.

A policeman, named Doc, was our traffic guard at school and the kids all loved him. Doc always had a pocketful of B-B bat taffies, or similar candy. He distributed these to the children on a daily basis, and he could always be found on duty at the Fourth of July celebration handing out his usual treats. The kids all flocked around him!

Fireworks were displayed after dark. After that all the children went home and the young adults remained for a time of dancing in the streets.

Labor Day, celebrated the first Monday in September, was generally set aside for a family picnic and preparing for the new school year which usually began several days later.

Columbus Day (October 12) was the first holiday celebrated in the fall. The schools always held a special assembly honoring Christopher Columbus and his contributions to our great country, and to the world.

Halloween, the last day of October, was usually celebrated in school in a low-key manner. Some years we were permitted to wear costumes to school and have a parade. Mostly it was left to the discretion of the individual teachers to decide how to handle the observance.

After dark, children in our neighborhood always dressed in costumes and went from door-to-door "trick or treating." The neighborhood was a very safe one and children could go anywhere within a large area and get bags and bags filled with candy, apples, cookies, pretzels, etc. Some more affluent neighbors would throw in a nickel, dime, or a quarter, which was a real treat in those days. Local stores were no exception. They always had a treat for the kids at Halloween.

Parents often recycled the goodies their children brought home because it was not unusual for them to run out of their own supply before the neighborhood children stopped coming for the evening, and there was always more than ample treats collected than any one family could consume.

Armistice Day, November 11, (now called Veterans Day) was celebrated by a moment of silence promptly at 11:11 a.m. We had special assemblies and took flags to school, which were collected by the American Legion to be placed on the graves of fallen military personnel.

Thanksgiving was a special holiday. The story of the pilgrims was repeated each year in school. One year we made dolls out of cloth representing both the Colonial Americans and the Indians, and re-enacted the scene. Turkeys, ears of corn, and leaves were made out of construction paper, which decorated the classrooms. We were always permitted to take them home for decoration and to share with our families for the holiday.

Many churches held Thanksgiving services at 8:00 a.m. before family activities began for the day.

It was Alumni Day at the high school in the 1940s, and many family members and neighbors attended the football game which was always the last one of the season.

Gimbel Brothers always staged a large parade with floats and balloons. The eagerly awaited arrival of Santa Claus appeared at the end of the parade. It was timed so that promptly at 12:00 noontime, Santa would climb a ladder and enter an upper story window of their department store at 9th and Market streets. This was the official opening of the Christmas shopping season, and the beginning of the countdown for the big awaited day.

At home Thanksgiving was celebrated as a "family" day. Our family always had a large turkey dinner with all the trimmings...banana and cranberry salad, mashed potatoes, candied sweet potatoes, peas, turkey, dressing, and, of course, pumpkin and mincemeat pies for dessert. Grandmother and Aunt Floss usually joined us for the feast. After dinner, we all played games...many times it was Monopoly once the game became more affordable and we were fortunate enough to receive one as a gift.

Christmas was celebrated in school prior to going on Christmas vacation. Older students went through the halls singing the many Christmas carols which we were taught and also sang in class, and there was always an exchange of cards between classmates. Pollyanna gifts were also exchanged. Each student selected the name of a classmate and purchased a gift costing between ten cents to twenty-five cents. Teachers always discreetly made certain there was a gift for every student. If one student couldn't afford to buy a gift, the teacher purchased the gift.

Christmas was a special time in our house. We snooped like most kids, and one year we found a number of very beautifully decorated boxes under our parents' bed. When we opened them and looked inside, all we found were flannel pajamas. What a disappointment! It was certainly not a gift any child would hope to find at Christmas.

Christmas Eve found us Christmas caroling with our friends. That was a wonderful experience...particularly on a crisp, cold winter night after a snowfall. When we finished caroling, we went to someone's home for cocoa and cake, or cookies, and an exchange of gifts. In addition, gifts were often exchanged with close friends, and, since we had a large family, we drew a name and bought a gift for one of our siblings. Mother usually helped with the gift selection.

Our family always had a real tree and wreaths were placed on the front door and in each window of the house. Lights were not used to decorate anything except the tree until the mid to late 1940s or early 1950s. Crepe paper and cardboard cutouts were used extensively. We even had a cardboard replica of a fireplace.

Stockings were always hung and Santa filled them with various goodies: candy, an apple, an orange, nail polish, a can of soup, and similar things.

Christmas morning we could not go downstairs until everyone was dressed. Then dad went down, turned on the lights, and stoked the furnace. The homes were heated by coal furnaces in those days. Then we had to line up. Mother went first, followed by the youngest, and then the next in line, according to age. The oldest, or firstborn, was always last. Each child had their own special place set aside which displayed their "gifts from Santa".

Though money was scarce, there were always plenty of gifts for each one of us. Each year we received many items including a "Lady Esther" manicure kit for the girls. This was a three inch by three inch yellow cardboard box that contained a bottle of clear (pink) nail polish, a bottle of nail polish remover, a little tin containing cuticle remover cream, an orange stick, and a wad of cotton. They were sold in the five and ten cents store for twenty-five cents each, as were many of our other gifts including socks, paper dolls, as well as coloring and various activity books that provided us with many pleasurable hours.

One Christmas we were thrilled to receive tricycles that, unknown to us, our dad had refurbished with new wheels, new seats, and a new paint job. To us they were new! We were thrilled!

Another year trunk dolls were the popular gift most little girls wanted to receive. My mother bought a doll and made clothes for it, and my dad made a trunk out of plywood. One side held the doll and the other side had hangers on which to hang the clothes, and there was a drawer at the bottom to store accessories like a comb, brush, hair ribbons, and shoes and socks belonging to the doll. Dad also made me a doll house and a wooden party table. No thought was ever given to the fact they were lovingly handmade and not store bought. We never knew the difference, nor did we care. We were always thrilled with whatever gifts we received.

Parents, out of necessity, had to be creative and did what they had to do to please their children so they wouldn't feel left out or neglected, and the gifts were always very much appreciated. They also had to do this within a very limited budget that they could not exceed. What a challenge that must have been for our parents with six children!

After everything was viewed, we gathered at the table for a breakfast of scrambled eggs, juice, and toast. When breakfast was cleared away, a pile of wrapped gifts was placed in front of each of us. As a matter of courtesy, we sat and watched each one open his or her gifts until everyone was finished. Then, it was off to visit friends to see the gifts they received.

During the period between Christmas and New Year's, it was customary to visit as many homes of family and friends as was possible. Gifts were not put away until New Year's Day, except for the new clothes that individuals chose to wear immediately.

Churches had Christmas parties with plays, recitations, and carol singing. Each family member who attended received an apple, an orange, and a box of hard candy.

Christmas was not as commercialized as it is today. The true meaning of Christmas was highly emphasized in the home, the churches and the schools.

Chapter 6
Household Chore Routine

Like most well-run businesses, households must have an organized routine to keep things running smoothly. Our home was no different. In addition to the daily chores, we had a schedule, and certain chores were assigned and performed on certain days of the week.

Monday was traditionally the major "laundry day." Washing machines were quite different then. They were not automatic. The washer had to be filled with water, before the clothes and detergent were added. Heavily soiled clothes were doused in water and the soiled area scrubbed with Fels-Naptha soap, and then rubbed against a corrugated metal scrub board or washboard. Then they were placed into the washing machine, which had an agitator in the center that rotated around the clothes to wash them. (Note: Fels-Naptha soap is brown in color, and comes in a bar shape. It was also used in the bath following a day in the woods to prevent ivy poison. It is still available in the stores today.)

When the washer stopped, the clothes were placed individually through a wringer at the top of the washer, and from there they went into a tub of clear water to rinse off the soap. Then they were put back through the wringer into a clothes basket before being taken to the backyard to be hung on the clothesline.

On a number of occasions, the story has been told that my oldest brother put his arm through the wringer. He was reportedly standing on a workbench by the washer so he could watch the activity, and mother could also keep her eye on him to keep him out of mischief. Being curious, I guess, he decided to place his hand and arm through the wringer when mother turned her back for a split second. That's all it took! Mother had to quickly turn off the washer and depress a lever which released the rollers on the wringer. Then she removed his arm and he was rushed to the hospital. His hand and arm were carefully bandaged because he had crushed some of the bones. He was quite active and known as an experimenter!

[Another time he swallowed a dime. My parents took him to the local drugstore and bought him a chocolate soda. When they returned home, he was as happy as a lark. He felt he had pulled one over on the rest of us because he got a chocolate soda and we didn't. Before long, we enjoyed the laugh because what he didn't know was that the chocolate soda contained castor oil.]

Clothes that needed to be starched were placed in another tub or bucket that contained a prepared starch mixture before being run through the wringer, and then they were placed into a clothes basket. From there they were carried outside to the backyard and hung on clotheslines to air dry. If you're wondering why the clothes weren't just put into either the electric or gas dryer to be dried, forget it! They didn't exist. Hanging clothes on the line in the yard provided neighbors an opportunity to visit with one another---thus, I guess the expression, "chatting over the backyard fence," was coined.

During the winter, and when the weather was inclement, the clothes were hung in the basement to dry.

Once dry, sheets were folded and carried either from the yard or from the basement, and then upstairs to the second floor bedroom area and placed back on the beds. Items like towels, socks, underwear, and other such things were folded and put away. The other items stayed in the laundry basket overnight. Houses did not have either linen closets or an abundance of storage places in those days so, by necessity, supplies of everything were very limited.

Tuesday was ironing day. The clothes that required ironing were sprinkled with water from an old ketchup bottle with a perforated cap, and ironed. They were either placed on hangers or put away in drawers.

Wednesday was sewing day. With a family of eight, there was always mending to be done, socks to be darned, or buttons to be sewn on. If there was spare time, baking could be done, clothes made, shopping, or visiting with friends and relatives.

Thursday was reserved for cleaning the upstairs area. We did not have wall-to-wall carpeting, so floors had to be mopped, furniture dusted, the bathroom thoroughly cleaned, etc.

Friday, the downstairs was thoroughly cleaned, area rugs vacuumed, throw rugs shaken outdoors, wooden floors mopped, and furniture dusted. Laundry was done again.

Saturday was always a busy day. It was shopping day, unless our parents were able to take care of that on Friday night. The kitchen and bathroom floors and cellar steps had to be scrubbed as well as the porch and the front steps.

Sidewalks had to be swept. Chores like window washing, tending to screens, and other seasonal tasks were also done on Saturday when the men and boys were home. Scrubbing was done the old fashioned way with a scrubbing brush, pail, and a can of Dutch Cleanser.

Sunday was the Sabbath Day," and our mother, having a Victorian upbringing, was very strict about observing it. We could not do any chores of any kind on Sunday. The only games we were permitted to play were Bible-related. We regularly attended Sunday school and church in the morning. When we got home, we had to change our clothes and have lunch, which usually consisted of sandwiches and/or soup and milk or Kool-Aid in the summer. Then we could take a walk, visit friends, play games, or just sit and chat. (Note: We had limited Sunday outfits, school outfits, and play clothes.)

Dinnertime usually found guests joining us---our aunt, and various friends from time to time. After dinner, it was back to church to attend the young people's group followed by evening worship. Young people's group always consisted of a hymn sing, and a review of past activities, as well as a discussion of future activities that were in the planning stages. We also talked about items of general interest to us at the particular time. Frequently we had guest speakers but there was never anything real heavy discussed, since it was more of a social gathering. Unlike today's groups, the group was not structured thematically nor did we have any specific topics to discuss. It was just a week-to-week happening—a place to go and something positive to do while interacting with our friends. Each participant took a turn at leading the group, and the selections were made based on what they and perhaps their closest friend or friends wanted to do or discuss.

Chapter 7
Potpourri of Memories

Reflecting on this period of my life has brought so many wonderful events to mind that I decided to briefly mention them to give you a broader glimpse. They all are precious memories and are not listed in any particular order. It was an exciting era and there was always something going on. There was absolutely no time for boredom.

The practice of hand-me-down clothes was common in those days. Having two older sisters, you can be sure I had more than my share, but I didn't complain. I felt lucky to have so many clothes, and my wardrobe also included some of the popular "Shirley Temple" dresses. My sisters often wore the same style dresses but in different colors, providing me with duplicates. (That probably accounts for the reason why today I will purchase the same outfit that I particularly like, in two or three different colors.) In addition, my sisters each had friends who were only children so I received their hand-me-downs also.

When the soles of our shoes developed holes, we placed pieces of cardboard inside them until our parents could get to the store and purchase replacement soles to cement on.

We recycled back then, too. Bread wrappers were carefully folded and used to wrap sandwiches for lunch. The ends of tin cans were removed manually with an old-fashion opener that was difficult to use. They were then washed, flattened by foot, and placed in receptacles to be recycled for re-use since metal was scarce due to the war.

When my oldest brother was seven-and-one-half years of age, he received a pair of storm boots that he had begged and begged for. There was a pocket on the side of one of the boots which held a pocketknife, and all the boys wanted these special boots. He had promised to be very careful with it, but one day he left the knife lying on his bed with the blade exposed. I was one-and-one-half years of age at the time, and, I suppose filled with curiosity, I picked up the knife. I've been told that I was rushed to St. Vincent's Hospital at 69th Street and Woodland Avenue, where my finger had to be stitched. My left index finger has a one inch diagonal scar on it so it must have been a good sized cut. We were not bad kids, but we were rambunctious and had high levels of energy.

The nurses at that time wore very impressive stiffly starched white uniforms, white hose, white shoes, and white caps which depicted their level of proficiency. Teens often volunteered at hospitals and wore striped uniforms with white pinafores and were known as "candy stripers." Depending on the individual hospital, some uniforms had red stripes and others had blue stripes.

The smell of ether permeated the air when you approached a hospital. That is the anesthetic that was primarily used in those days, and it left an unforgettable aroma etched in one's memory.

Visits to doctors' offices cost $2.00 and doctors dispensed pills in little envelopes on which they wrote the instructions pertaining to the dosage and times the pills were to be taken. Doctors also made house calls back then. I believe the fee charged was $5.00 for a house call. They carried little black bags containing items like their stethoscope, tongue depressor, thermometer, hypodermic needle, alcohol, cotton balls, prescription pads and whatever else they thought they needed. One of my sisters told me that she always thought the doctor brought the new babies in his little black bag, because after the doctor left she heard the baby cry and our father came out and told the kids they had a new brother or sister. I also remember mother telling me that Chloroform was used as an anesthetic for the delivery when I was born.

One of the gifts girl friends exchanged with each other was a link with the giver's first name engraved on it. The links were about one inch long, made of either silver or pewter, and embossed with forget-me-nots around the edge. They were placed on a black grosgrain ribbon and tied around one's wrist until enough links were gathered to make a bracelet. Then the links were taken to Strawbridge's and linked together, a fastener added, and the recipient had a lovely bracelet, which made a cherished keepsake.

Spring brought many interesting people and activities to the area. A dog named "Nehi" visited the schools every year to teach safety rules for the children. Postcards with Nehi's picture were sent to each child following the visit to serve as a reminder of the safety rules.

An organ grinder with a monkey also visited the neighborhood. If we held a coin in our hand, the monkey would jump off the box, take the coin from our hand, jump back on the box, and put the coin in the slot. Then he would doff his hat. That was the signal for the organ grinder, who then cranked the box and played music. Oh, what fun that was for city kids to watch! They didn't come often enough to please us.

A man with a pony came around and took pictures of the children sitting on the pony, after which he visited the homes and tried to coerce parents into purchasing the pictures.

The circus and carnivals came to the fields and brought a group of people with them referred to as "gypsies."

Summer also brought a number of other interesting people and activities. A man driving a truck with a small merry-go-round on the back came by, and children could have rides for a penny or two. That was fun and we always looked forward to it as trips to amusement parks were rare and costly those days and they were not easily accessible.

A man known as "the waffle man" came by on a truck and made hot waffles. He covered them with white powdered sugar and sold them for ten cents each, or three for twenty-five cents. They were sure tasty!

Flavored water ice was sold at local corner stores in paper cone-shaped cups for two cents each. That was a real yummy treat! Italian water ice would probably be a close comparison.

We also had daily visits from the popsicle/ice cream and water ice vendors. They played loud music to signal their arrival so all the kids could gather. That was a real treat and very welcome on a hot summer night, when we could afford it. The loud music was not appreciated by young mothers who were trying to get their children asleep for their daily naps and at bedtime.

Before the introduction of plastic swimming pools, children played under the hose to cool down during hot summer periods. Some youngsters would turn on the fire hydrant at the corner and play under that until the police came and shut it off. The water pressure in the city got very low and they were concerned there would not be enough water to put out a fire should one develop.

Youngsters got together and played "school" to keep their skills sharp. Practicing reading, writing, civics, and math were favorites. We memorized the "times tables" and practiced fractions, and, as a result, we had a good foundation and were proficient in spelling and a number of other basic skills.

Temperatures in Philadelphia were often in the high nineties with high humidity ratings. Because of the terrible heat, in the evenings people sat out on the steps in an attempt to cool off, to supervise the children at play, and to visit with neighbors. There was no air conditioning in those days---and it was really HOT!

The older kids brought cattails from the fields and dried them out. We called them "punks" and they were lit with matches to ward off mosquitoes. Mosquitoes flew everywhere in the evenings and they gave mean bites which left large welts on the body. The cattails were later replaced by thinner manufactured sticks, and it was never proven whether or not they did any good. The kids thought they helped in keeping the mosquitoes away and it kept them amused.

Neighbors found different ways to be entertained. I remember one neighbor who decided to show films in his yard. People gathered and sat on the front steps and lawns until someone complained. When the authorities checked, the neighbor had not taken out the required permit so he could not continue with the show. You can be sure the neighbor who complained lost popularity with the rest of us....particularly the kids.

Warm, soft pretzels were always available and a big treat in Philadelphia. They are also one of the trademarks of the area.

The Elmwood Cadets, a local band of teenagers, paraded up and down the streets in full uniform. This gave them an opportunity to practice their drills for performances at various community affairs, and also provided entertainment for the neighborhood. They were fun to watch as we knew many of them from school, church, and the neighborhood.

The lamplighter came by late every afternoon, climbed his ladder, and lit the gas lights in front of our houses. These were later replaced by electric lights.

Root beer was a popular drink, and every summer Dad made it for our family. It was quite an involved process. After the bottles were filled, they had to be laid out on the roof top for a period of weeks to fully age. Root beer and pretzels were among the favorite refreshments served when families got together for visits with one another. (It also provided an excuse for my oldest brother to climb up on the roof, as that was generally not a permitted activity, and, of course, it was something he liked to do and did at every given opportunity.)

A neighbor cooked a chicken one Saturday evening for Sunday dinner. She placed it on the back porch to cool before refrigerating it. When she went to get it to put it away, it was gone. Reportedly, it was found with other items that had disappeared from the neighborhood---including clothes taken from a clothesline---in the house of another neighbor, who was later identified as a "kleptomaniac."

During summer vacation, the schools opened the playgrounds for recreational purposes. The day began with an assembly where the flag was raised and saluted, and we sang fun songs and heard a story. Words to the songs were printed in large letters on large pieces of poster board, so we could all learn them and sing them together. Free time to play on the equipment, or to participate in arts and crafts or games, was then made available. There was also a closing program at the end of the day.

Once a year, the neighbors on some of the streets would rope off blocks for a "block party". Game booths were set up and the neighbors all enjoyed mingling, eating and playing various games with one another. That was an exciting time for all because the entire neighborhood came alive and we had an opportunity to play games like those featured on the boardwalk at the New Jersey shore. We were also able to win prizes like big teddy bears, dolls, etc.

In the fall everyone looked forward to the visit of the priests from the local parishes. At that time they would call on the parishioners and tell the families what their contributions to the church were expected to be for the coming year. It was a big event for the entire neighborhood, whether they were a member of that particular church or not.

Diseases like mumps, measles, German measles, chicken pox, scarlet fever, polio, spinal meningitis, etc. were considered very contagious and dangerous in those days. The entire household was quarantined and signs were posted on the front door. No one was permitted to enter or leave the house until the board of health removed the sign. That period usually lasted from ten to twenty-one days, depending on the nature and severity of the disease.

When someone who lived on the street died, it was a community event because everyone knew everyone and cared about them. Crepes of either gray or black ribbon were placed on the door, depending on the age of the deceased.

The hearse arrived to remove the body. Next, several days later, trucks would arrive delivering chairs to the house, followed by the florist with potted palms and floral arrangements. The crepe on the door was then replaced with a floral spray, and the undertaker would return the body, which had been prepared for viewing, the service, and burial.

At the appointed time, the neighbors would enter the house for the viewing and funeral service. Neighbors knew everyone in the community and were very supportive of one another and treated each other as family.

The children called the neighbors by name—Mr. or Mrs.—or, in cases where there was an extremely close bond between the families, they addressed the adults as aunt or uncle.

Sharing what we had with others was instilled in us at a very early age, and we were taught to contribute pennies, nickels, and dimes whenever we could to help those who were less fortunate than we were.

The schools held fund-raisers to help in coordinating the activities of various organizations. In the spring, to coincide with the anniversary of President Franklin Delano Roosevelt's birthday, the students were each asked to bring a dime to contribute to the March of Dimes, an organization which was established in 1938. President Roosevelt was afflicted with infantile paralysis, which is today known as polio. The money donated was used for research and treatment to help stamp out this dreadful disease. The Salk vaccine, which was given both orally and by injection, is an example of one of the results of the research done with money donated to this very worthy organization.

The American Red Cross also sponsored drives in the spring, and the proceeds went to help families and service personnel with various needs. Each student received a button or lapel pin in exchange for their contribution. Contests were held between the classes to determine which class collected the most money. It was customary to hold a recognition honoring that particular class.

At the beginning of Lent, the churches passed out cardboard banks in the shape of a church. Each person was asked to put three cents per day into the bank, representing one cent for each of the three meals they ate during the forty day Lenten period. The banks were then returned to church on Easter Sunday and the money donated was used to provide food for the hungry.

Prior to Memorial Day, veterans stood on street corners and outside of stores and exchanged red artificial poppies for donations, just as they do today. The poppies were proudly worn by all who received them because they knew that, by doing so, their contributions were helping the wounded veterans who served our country. It was also a way of showing patriotism, and of expressing gratitude to them.

Canned goods were collected for the needy between the period immediately before Thanksgiving through Christmas, both at the schools and in the churches.

Electric refrigerators were not household items in those days. Foods were refrigerated in wooden ice boxes which were cooled by blocks of ice purchased at nearby ice houses. It was often the chore of the children to go to the corner ice house, purchase the block of ice, and take it home—usually in a wagon. Blocks of ice cost ten cents, fifteen cents, or twenty-five cents, depending on the size of the block. The ice, of course, melted, and there was a compartment in the bottom of the ice box to hold a galvanized pan to collect the water. This had to be emptied on a regular basis.

At special times, such as Thanksgiving, when extra food had to be bought, stored, and prepared ahead of time, it was customary to place the food in galvanized steel window boxes that sat on the window sill outside the dining room window.

Refrigerators began to replace ice boxes in the late 1930s and early 1940s. We got our first electric refrigerator at the onset of World War II. The butter keeper was on order, but due to war priorities, it never became available. We did have ice cube trays, and, with our particular model refrigerator, we had the capability of making ice cubes, popsicles (made from juice and/or Kool-Aid), and ice cream. What a wonderful invention that was! It was a great convenience and provided us with many new advantages. The downside though was the weekly defrosting chore. That was truly a chore everyone disliked. Ugh! It was time consuming and a very messy chore.

The Southwest Globe Times which covered news items pertaining to the people and organizations within the community was distributed, free of charge, on a weekly basis.

Chapter 8
Schools

Schools of all levels were in walking distance to our home, which provided a great opportunity to develop friendships among our classmates, and also was a great form of exercise. In our immediate area, there were several elementary schools (grades K-6), a junior high school (grades 7-9), and later, in 1939, a high school was built (grades 9-12)

My siblings and I attended John M. Patterson Elementary School at 70th Street and Buist Avenue; William T. Tilden Junior High School at 66th Street and Elmwood Avenue; and John Bartram High School at 67th Street and Elmwood Avenue.

In junior high school we learned home economics, covering basic cleaning, cooking and sewing skills, which equipped us for the future. The basics of sewing taught us how to use a sewing machine with a treadle. In sewing class we made bags in which to carry our sewing supplies as well as napkins, tea towels, a blouse, and a skirt.

Saving pennies, nickels, dimes, and quarters and investing them in an interest-earning savings account was also introduced to us in junior high school. Representatives from the Philadelphia Savings Fund Society (also known as PSFS) visited our school on Mondays to encourage our involvement.

Each class selected a bank teller who was responsible to collect the funds, fill out the deposit slips, and write a receipt for the student investor. Each investor received a passbook into which the deposits and interest were recorded by the bank and returned to the students the following week. I had the honor of serving as a teller, which was fun and taught me responsibility for detail.

The local high school (John Bartram) was opened in 1939. That was an exciting event for everyone. Prior to its opening, students had to take public transportation or be driven to other areas for their high school education. The only other option was to drop out of school and seek employment, which was difficult at that time since jobs for unskilled workers were very scarce.

There were also several local parochial schools which provided education through grade 8. The local ones in our immediate neighborhood were St. Barnabas, St. Clements, St. Mary's and Our Lady of Loretta. After completing the elementary program, the students had the option of attending a public high school or taking public transportation to another area to attend a parochial high school.

Students from an expanded area throughout the city merged into Bartram High School because it was new and offered a variety of interesting activities and experiences for everyone. In addition, the school also had high academic standards, and was administered by a very capable and popular principal---Dr. Wesley E. Scott---who was much beloved by all.

The high schools offered three basic curriculums: Academic for those planning to attend college; Commercial for students planning a business or retail career; and Vocational for students interested in trade careers.

Some students had the opportunity to work part time and attend school part time providing them with actual hands-on experience enabling them to develop specific skills and knowledge in preparation for employment after graduation.

Although I was not enrolled in this program, I did work part time. During the summer vacation, after school and on Saturdays, I had the opportunity to work in a Horn & Hardart retail store on Woodland Avenue. Horn & Hardart was one of the largest employers in the Philadelphia area.

Through this job I had the opportunity to develop many business-related skills, such as dealing with people, customer relations, handling cash transactions, order taking, inventory control, etc.

Horn & Hardart was a baking company and operated restaurants, cafeterias, retail stores, and automats in the Philadelphia and surrounding areas. Automats were known by kids as the "nickel eating house". In the automat one could select whatever food item was desired, put nickels in a slot, open a glass door, and remove the selected food item. The pay was forty cents per hour and the employees received a 25 percent discount on purchases. Among other foods, they were well known for their scrumptious pumpkin pie and sticky cinnamon buns, for which I have not found any comparison. The recipes for these and other items for which they were famous have never been made available as far as I know.

The day before Thanksgiving every year customers began to line up outside the store and around the block, beginning at 6:00 a.m., to pick up preordered items and/or to purchase pies and other desired items for their Thanksgiving dinner. The shelves at the store were completely bare by 3:00 p.m.

At Christmas the company held large parties for the children of all employees. The parties were held in a major hotel in downtown Philadelphia. They always had an enjoyable program and each child had a chance to personally talk with and to receive a gift from Santa, and refreshments were served to everyone in attendance. Because of the practice of segregation which was in effect at the time, and to accommodate the number of children involved, they held two identical parties: one in the morning and one in the afternoon.

There was a real disappointment and loss felt throughout the city when Horn & Hardart closed their doors and ceased to operate.

High school introduced us to competitive sports: bowling, football, basketball, and softball. Attending pep rallies and games were fun and exciting experiences. Our basketball teams (aptly named the "Whiz Kids") were exceptional and played many games at the Palestra, the University of Pennsylvania stadium.

There was a great deal of enthusiasm, and spirit at the school ran very high because of the great interaction between the home, the community, and the school.

We had a school newspaper called the "Jay Bee." It was published every Monday and cost five cents. Everyone eagerly looked forward to the next issue as we thoroughly enjoyed reading it.

The yearbook was called "The Trailmarker," and, unlike today, it was only available to members of the senior graduating class.

The school store, at which I was privileged to work, sold spirit items as well as school supplies and tickets to the various school activities.

On days when our teams played, most students wore outfits consisting of the school colors, which were maroon and gray. We also sported large school pins with maroon and gray ribbons hanging from them. Our bobby sox had the year of our graduation appliquéd on them.

Fashionable outfits for the girls included dresses, and skirts worn with blouses and/or sweaters. In this era, full skirts with crinolines worn under them were in vogue.

With dressy skirts we wore jesters, prior to the introduction of Roman sandals, and with casual attire we wore bobby sox and saddle shoes. Jesters were little flat slip-on shoes and were available in black suede and white, brown, or black leather. Saddle shoes were available in combinations of either brown and white or black and white. Sneakers were only worn during gym class. They had to be white—and clean.

We also wore little flippy bows pinned in our hair with either bobby pins or little metal clips. The colors matched or complemented our outfits. They were considered chic.

It was considered inappropriate for the girls to wear shorts, culottes, slacks, or jeans to school in those days. The only exception was for the cheerleaders, who wore culottes as part of their school-approved uniform. These were permitted to be worn on special occasions, and on days when games were to be played and the cheerleaders were scheduled to perform.

Girls did wear gym suits on days when they had physical education, but they either had to be changed before leaving the gym, or a skirt worn over them in class.

Shorts, rompers, and one piece playsuits were worn by the girls in the summer for play, but never for school.

Boys wore regular slacks and shirts. In the 1930s they wore knickers. They, too, wore shorts in the summer for play.

The underlying thought behind the unwritten dress code was that performance was influenced by the way people dressed. If people dressed nicely, they would take pride in themselves and also in what they did, and, of course, the outcome would be neater and more proficient.

Each spring our drama classes put on plays which were outstanding and received great public support. We had lots of great talent in our area and some of our classmates and other members of the alumni went on to enjoy great professional careers in movies, on Broadway, and on TV.

Bartram High also had an outstanding music program. We had both an a cappella choir and a chorus. One May, our chorus had the honor of singing in the Philadelphia Municipal Stadium. That was a very memorable event. Choral groups from all high schools in the Philadelphia area participated, along with special performances by James Melton and other notable stars. It was a warm spring evening, and the event closed with a match-lighting ceremony which was absolutely breathtaking when all the lights were dimmed.

Thanksgiving was homecoming day in the 1940s after the high school began operation. Many alumni members came home and attended the annual football game. The following evening there was an informal gathering at the school which was open to all alumni. It was fun and we looked forward to gathering together and recalling memories with former classmates and friends. Some had moved away from the area or were away at college or in the military, and it was a pleasant experience to get together and catch up with one another.

We attended many wonderful assembly programs. One awe-inspiring assembly I fondly recall featured a visit by Miss America 1945---Bess Myerson. She was truly a beautiful young woman and a gifted pianist.

In addition to her beauty and talent, we were told that, during the final performance of the talent judging of the Miss America Pageant that year, Miss Myerson chose to stay away. Instead of making that appearance, she visited a group of wounded service personnel and performed for them. This reportedly won the hearts of the judges. She was indeed a wonderful role model and set an excellent example for all during the period of her reign.

Classes were graduated in both January and June back then. Each graduating class held an informal dinner dance at McAllister's in downtown Philadelphia. The June and January classes merged for the annual day trip to Washington, DC.

Each class held their own separate "class day". Our particular class held their class day activities at Drexel Lodge in Delaware County, just prior to graduation. These were all fun and carefree experiences, and created many wonderful memories for all who participated.

The class of January 1949, of which I was a member, had 252 members. *"Dinah's 49'ers"* was our class theme and we had a class song written by two of the class members. We also wore buttons with the drawing of Dinah from the 'Lil Abner Dog Patch era, featuring the class motif. Many of us had been classmates since kindergarten, and parting was indeed sweet sorrow. As with previous classes some of the students went to college, some were married and moved away, and some of the young men went into the military. The fond memories do linger on, and it is always rewarding when renewed contact is made between former classmates, even to this day.

Chapter 9
Shopping

Large supermarkets, like the Giant Tiger and Big Bear, were located in outlying areas and required transportation to get there. Family shopping was usually done on Friday evenings and Saturdays. Pennsylvania was a blue law state and stores were not permitted to conduct business of any kind on Sunday.

Bread was delivered by a horse-drawn wagon. There were two major bakeries in the city—Bond and Freihofers. The bread man also delivered cake, rolls, and donuts on order for very special occasions. Mother enjoyed baking and made these items for us on a regular basis so we generally did not take advantage of that feature. Mr. Wright was our delivery man. One of his daughters was a classmate of mine.

Milk was also delivered to our house by a horse-drawn wagon. There were two main dairies in the city which made home deliveries—Abbotts and Aristocrat. Aristocrat had a catchy slogan that has stuck with me over the years: "Angel child was once a brat 'til mother served Aristocrat."

In the winter, on very cold days, the cream would separate from the milk and rise to the top of the bottle causing the round cardboard lid to pop. That created a topic of conversation throughout the neighborhood.

Jimmy O'Neil delivered our milk. He was a man full of fun and had two children the ages of my oldest sister and brother. He was a neighborhood favorite. In the summer, we excitedly awaited his arrival as he would give us chips of ice which were used to help cool us down.

At times he would come into our house and play the piano and sing for us. Two tunes I remember him playing and singing were: "I can't get them up" and "I love coffee, I love tea, I love the girls, but they don't love me."

Bread and butter were also delivered by Mr. Bob of Bob's Better Butter and Eggs.

At the close of World War II, the horse-drawn wagons were replaced by motorized vehicles, and, as local shopping centers began to spring up, the home deliveries ended.

More and larger food markets were built locally and provided us with more shopping choices. ACME, A&P, Food Fair, and the Baltimore Markets came into existence.

There was a shopping district within walking distance on Woodland Avenue, between 62nd and 64th Streets. Going to the "Avenue" was always a fun outing because of the vast diversity of specialty shops, dry goods stores, millinery shops, men's and women's clothing stores, baby shops, shoe stores, furniture stores, pet shops, drugstores, Horn & Hardart retail store, 5 and 10 cent stores (Woolworth's, Newberrys, McCrory's, Greens, Grants, and Murphy's all competed for our business.), banks, movie theaters, etc. The floors of the butcher shops were always covered with sawdust.

If we couldn't find what we wanted at the "Avenue," we could hop a "J" bus and ride out to 69th and Market Streets, where there were more specialty shops and several larger department stores: Gimbel Brothers, Lit Brothers, Frank & Seder, and JC Penney.

Major shopping for items like clothing, accessories, and furniture was often done in downtown Philadelphia, also referred to as center city. Major upscale department stores like John Wanamaker, Strawbridge & Clothier, Gimbel Brothers, and Bonwit Tellers were located there.

The Reading Terminal was located at 12th and Market Streets, along with many specialty shops which provided a vast line of various kinds of merchandise.

One could spend all day shopping in "downtown Philadelphia." It was a "dress-up" occasion and women proudly wore hats and gloves when they went downtown.

A famous meeting place was at the "Eagle" in the center of the first floor of John Wanamaker's department store. It was a large bronze eagle in a large open area making it conducive for meeting people. We frequently met friends there when getting together for lunch or dinner, followed by shopping or a movie. Daily concerts were performed there at noon on the large pipe organ. Listening to the organ playing was an enjoyable and uplifting experience in itself. Macy's operates a department store at that location today, and it is my understanding that they still have the daily organ concerts.

During the period between Thanksgiving and Christmas, the windows of the department stores had beautiful decorations which were beyond imagination, and it was fun, and many times breathtaking, to go just to view them.

Each year between Thanksgiving and Christmas, one evening was always set aside for a family outing to go downtown to visit Santa Claus and to view the various displays there. That was truly a magical sight to behold, and we always looked forward to that outing.

The major department stores always had a fabulous toyland, and a visit there with Santa was a must. By the time we made this journey my siblings and I had carefully devoured the "Billy & Ruth" and Sears toy catalogs, which usually arrived around Thanksgiving. When the time arrived for our annual family outing, we had our wish list well memorized and ready to present to Santa during that special visit. In return, he always gave us a candy cane and an activity book which we always looked forward to receiving.

Some stores displayed large plush animated figures and staged special events, like "Punch & Judy" puppet shows for the children. It was an outing that we always looked forward to and enjoyed immensely as the shows and displays changed from year-to-year.

Many stores had very elaborate train layouts which everyone looked forward to seeing. We had a platform and electric trains at home which were set up every year at Christmastime, but our set-up did not compare to the displays in the department stores. They were beyond imagination, with several trains going through mountains, tunnels, and villages which were set at various levels. It was a real joy for young and old alike to see, particularly with the lights and sound effects.

Chapter 10
Transportation

The area in Southwest Philadelphia where we lived was conveniently located. We could walk to nearly every place we needed or wanted to go.

Automobiles were scarce and traveled only fifteen to twenty-five mph, and were used primarily on weekends, for emergencies, and for special occasions. Some autos had to be hand cranked to start the engine.

Visiting areas outside our own community often became a day's outing because many people did not have cars and the trip often required taking several trolleys and/or busses. Also, cars did not perform as they do today, and the roads were not as accommodating. My father had a 1929 Chevrolet, which was replaced by a gray 1936 Plymouth, followed by a black 1948 Ford, and later a 1954 green Plymouth.

Most houses did not have garages and the streets were very narrow and widely used by children at play, so on-street parking was neither feasible nor a good option at that time.

Dad's employer had several rows of garages adjacent to their facilities and he was fortunate enough to be able to rent one for $15/month. Going to the garage to get the car, or to put it away, was a big deal for us kids! We had to take turns with that and also with being able to sit "by a window" —a much coveted spot any time the family took a drive...

Aviation was in its infancy and very limited until World War II. Transporting military personnel, supplies, and equipment created the need for that industry and it began to grow. In the late 1940s, individuals who had learned to pilot planes during the war continued their interest, and small aircraft became popular and more accessible. Small fields opened up in outlying areas of the city to accommodate private pilots of small planes, and the larger airports also grew to accommodate the needs of the airlines which were beginning to expand and opened up a new mode of transportation. People were then able to visit other areas of the country in a relatively short period of time, and it became a real novelty and thrilling to fly to different places.

Children of all ages were thrilled to visit local airports to witness the expansions, and to watch airplanes—big and small—come in for a landing and take-off again.

Boats - The Delaware River flows from north to south and separates Pennsylvania from the state of New Jersey. Philadelphia, Pennsylvania and Camden, New Jersey are both prominent waterfront cities.

Barges, freighters, oil tankers and other vessels of all sizes and shapes could be observed on the water as they provided an integral means of transporting people, goods, equipment, food, materials and other supplies up, down and across the river to their destination.

Motorists who did not want to drive their automobiles across the Delaware River Bridge had the option of driving their cars onto a ferry boat which transported them to the other side along with passengers. This was also a fun trip for kids.

The Wilson Line ran cruise ships to and from Philadelphia, Pennsylvania and Wilmington, Delaware. There was also a cruise ship which transported people from Philadelphia to Pennsbury, New Jersey. Once there people could disembark and enjoy a day's outing at Riverview—an amusement park.

Busses, Els and Trolleys - The Philadelphia Transit Co (also known as the PTC) ran busses, els (an overhead train), and trolleys within the city limits. The trolleys ran on tracks in the center of the streets. On Elmwood Avenue there was the Route 36 trolley, which ran from Island Road to Front and Market Streets in downtown Philadelphia. On Woodland Avenue Routes 11, 12, and 37 trolleys ran from Darby to downtown Philadelphia via the subway. There was also the Route 13 trolley, which ran on Chester Avenue in the Yeadon area by Cobbs Creek.

Also there was a "G" bus which ran around 62nd Street, providing transportation to the Philadelphia Naval Shipyard. Connections and transfers could be made between the various vehicles. Some trolleys went into the subway (underground). There was also the elevated train (known as the "el") which ran from 69th and Market Street east to center city via the subway and then north to the Frankford area.

If you rode the "el" from the beginning of the line at 69th and Market Streets to the other end of the line at Frankford, you could enjoy a ride overhead as well as under the ground all in one trip, and vice versa. That was a particularly fun ride for the children.

The cost to ride the PTC was one token, which available from the conductor or motorman on board the vehicle at a cost of two for fifteen cents. Some transfers were free; others cost a few cents.

These vehicles ran on a regular and frequent schedule. There used to be a saying: "Trolleys and busses are like men.

If you miss one, don't fret, there is always another one coming down the line, or just around the bend."

The Red Arrow line also ran busses from 67th Street and Elmwood Avenue to 69th and Market Streets (the "J" bus) and beyond. At 69th and Market Streets there was a large terminal where people could connect with other busses and/or trolleys, and the "el," to travel to other outlying areas throughout Delaware County, Paoli, and West Chester. A ride on the Red Arrow vehicle cost ten cents or you could purchase tickets at a cost of three for twenty-five cents.

Another firm ran an open-sided trolley, called the Liberty Bell. That was a fun and scenic ride as it wound its way through wooded and undeveloped areas!

Trains - In addition, the Pennsylvania Railroad, Reading Railroad, and the Baltimore & Ohio Railroad all provided train transportation through the city to suburban areas, north to New York and beyond, south to Florida, and west to other destinations. Trains were popular and very crowded especially during the periods of time when the PTC went on strike. They provided the best available method for people to reach their places of employment. Freight trains were also widely used to transport materials, coal and other items.

Chapter 11
Vacations

Family vacations were few and far between due to work and various other schedules, or illness of family members, funding, and other reasons. Since Philadelphia is rich in history and William Penn, the founder of Philadelphia and Pennsylvania, is a distant relative, the significance and value of this history and our heritage was deeply instilled in us at a very young age. We visited the various historical places such as Betsy Ross's house, Independence Hall, the Liberty Bell, and Elfreth's Alley.

There is a large bronze statue of William Penn at the top of City Hall. Prior to World War II, visitors to City Hall could ride an elevator to the top of the building and, I've been told, could stand on the brim of his hat. I recall hearing the width of the brim spanned six feet across, and one could see the entire city and surrounding areas from that vista. We were also told that, at one time, there was an unwritten rule that no building in the city could exceed the height of this statue. I believe that has since been changed.

William Penn was a Quaker and he was a firm believer in practicing the Golden Rule, which was the basis of our upbringing.

Occasionally we took day trips to the zoo and to the aquarium, where I recall seeing a mammoth size turtle reportedly to be 100 years old. There also was an electric eel with a warning sign posted on the tank that visitors should be careful not to touch the glass.

We visited the art museum and other places of interest like the Franklin Institute. The Franklin Institute houses many scientific and technical exhibits and you can spend days there taking in all the wonderful displays, and probably not see everything. The Fels Planetarium is part of the Franklin Institute, and every year around Christmas they had a special showing that incorporated the Star of Bethlehem. [The planetarium was named for Samuel Fels, a philanthropist, who was president of the Fels Manufacturing Company, located at 73rd Street and Island Road, adjacent to Cobbs Creek. The company made laundry soap and they provided funding for the planetarium.]

One or two summers my parents rented a cottage on the Perkiomen Creek at Collegeville. That provided a fun and carefree vacation which the entire family enjoyed. The respite provided freedom from our daily chores and we could spend the entire day out-of-doors, primarily swimming in the creek. In the evenings we played board games as a family. The small-town environment was a welcome change from the city.

When we were old enough, we were permitted to go to camp. One such camp I recall attending several summers was Camp Sankanac which was situated on the French Creek. Learning 300 Bible verses in Bible club earned children the privilege of attending camp for one week free of charge.

Activities there included daily devotions, cabin cleaning contests, arts and crafts, swimming, boating, skits, and games. Many growth experiences were enjoyed there and left me with cherished memories. One song that we learned that has stayed with me through the years was called "J-O-Y" and it was sung to the tune of "Jingle Bells." The gist of the message is that if, in your life, you make a practice of putting Jesus first, yourself last, and others in between, true joy could be experienced . I don't know who wrote the lyrics but they are:

J-O-Y! J-O-Y!
This must surely mean
Jesus first,
Yourself last, and
Others in between.

(The lyrics are repeated a second time.)

Another song (currently in public domain) we sang at mealtime was:

"Morning (Noontime, Evening as appropriate) is here,
The board is spread, thanks be to God
Who gives us bread."

Also, I attended Camp Rohrman, on the Brandywine Creek in Downingtown, one summer. I did not care as much for that camp as it was less structured and not religious in nature.

As teenagers we went to Camp Ockanickon at Medford Lakes, New Jersey, with other Christian Endeavor groups throughout Philadelphia. At the time, the premises were owned by the Y.M.C.A. and leased to various groups during periods when the camp was not in operation. The setting was on many acres and had Indian totem poles, etc. set among tall pines and man-made lakes. Meetings were held outdoors in an area called the "sugar bowl."

Roasting hot dogs and marshmallows around an evening campfire on the sandy shore of the lake, followed by a songfest, created a most memorable and inspiring experience.

We also participated in a silent communion service in the outdoor open-air chapel in the woods, which helped us to appreciate worship surrounded by nature at its best. All participants were asked to enter and to leave in silence. That was a truly awesome and most impressive experience!

Medford Lakes is a very beautiful spot and very dear to my heart. My friends and I have many fond memories of times spent there.

A community of log cabins surrounds the camp, and I always thought it would be an ideal place to live. Many doctors and business executives owned these cabins, and used them as second homes or places of retreat on weekends and during the summer. I had a friend who made her year-round home there. It is, in my opinion, truly "paradise on Earth."

Part II
World War II and its Effects

December 7, 1941, familiarly known as "Pearl Harbor Day", is indeed a day that will live in infamy! I have vivid memories of hearing President Roosevelt's famous announcement on radio as my parents, some of my siblings and I sat in our living room that evening. The announcement gave us many things to ponder and wonder about. Many changes occurred in the days, weeks and months that followed as the result of that event, and those changes greatly affected the lives of everyone living in America.

Chapter 12
Changes Resulting From World War II

This was indeed a time when every person, in every household, was affected in some way. It was a difficult time for all and had lasting effects on the entire country. Our neighborhood in Southwest Philadelphia was no exception.

Fathers, uncles, brothers, cousins, and neighbors soon began receiving notices to report to the local draft board for physical examinations and classification. Many of them were drafted into various branches of the military and went off to war. Others enlisted as did many women to serve in the WACS (Army), WAMS (Marines), WAVES (Navy), WAFS (Air Force), SPARS (Women's Coast Guard Reserve), or the Red Cross. Some who were not accepted by the military joined the Civil Air Patrol (CAP). Many teachers were included, and older women were hired to take their places in the schools to continue providing education for the youngsters. Everyone did what they could to help their country at this difficult time.

Many families moved to the city from western Pennsylvania and other areas to seek employment in the defense industries where jobs became plentiful. Defense plants operated three shifts around the clock, seven days a week, to produce the necessary items needed by the military.

Apartment complexes were built to provide housing for the influx of people. Bartram's Garden was one area where such a complex was built. Large red brick buildings were constructed on the grassy acres to accommodate the influx of new residents to the area.

Families placed small banners in their front windows to honor those who were serving in the military. The banner had a blue star in the center of a white background for each member of that family actively serving. It was surrounded by a red border, and edged with gold fringe. One family up the street had five stars representing their five sons who were serving. Patriotism was widespread throughout the city. Young families moved in with grandparents to provide in-house child care and to reduce living costs, since many young mothers were forced to go to work to feed, clothe, and provide for their children. Some were unskilled and took whatever jobs were available in banks, stores, hospitals, and factories. Some of the women who worked in factories were given the title "Rosie the Riveter." Schools opened up to provide training to help people develop needed skills.

Bond rallies were commonplace. School children were encouraged to save money and to buy war bonds. Each person was given booklets into which they could paste stamps. They were much like the ones used by trading stamp companies which were given as premiums for certain purchases. It cost $18.75 to purchase a bond that would eventually be worth $25 because of the interest it would earn if held until maturity. Bonds could be purchased outright or people could buy stamps for ten cents and twenty-five cents each, and save them until the booklet was full. Full books could be redeemed for a $25 bond. Bonds were also available in $50 (cost $37.50) and larger denominations.

Payroll deductions to purchase bonds were encouraged and made available at most places of employment. Participation in this program was a way in which everyone could support the troops and the overall war effort in a search for peace.

The USO opened canteens to entertain service personnel and to provide a taste of home for them during their leave times. They served coffee and donuts, and carefully screened hostesses were available to talk to and dance with the GIs. The big band era was in full swing and the music of that era became very popular, and, in my opinion, remains unparalleled.

Schools had special assemblies honoring the military personnel. Bartram High had a flag in memory of each of her sons and daughters who gave their lives in service to the country. That was a moving and impressive experience when they were displayed and when the honor roll of names called at community and special school events!

Movie producers began to produce family-oriented musicals in color. News documentaries became a part of every show, and most shows included cartoons, which everyone enjoyed.

Blackout drills were conducted frequently in every neighborhood. Sirens would blare unexpectedly, and people had to pull down black window shades and put out the lights until the "all-clear" siren sounded.

Each block had a team of air raid wardens who were equipped with an arm band for identification, a hard helmet, a whistle, and a flashlight. Their main responsibility was to patrol up and down the block to ensure everyone complied with the rules and was safe. At times one could be heard calling, "Get those lights out!"

In school we also had drills. We had to crawl under the desk and sit quietly until the drill was over. That action was called "duck and cover".

We had pen pals encouraged by teachers. Names were taken from magazines like *Weekly Reader* and *Calling all Girls.* There were three or four different girls in England with whom I exchanged letters, cards, and gifts for several years. The letters were censored and certain words were cut out or blackened before we received them. This was typical of mail being sent to and from countries as well as the United States, and was done to provide security to prevent secrets from being divulged that could be harmful to our national security.

The military had priority when it came to supplies, and many items became unavailable or could only be purchased in limited quantities. Many things were rationed. Each family received a ration book of coupons for each member of the household. The coupons determined what items and what quantity of each item could be purchased. This also included gasoline for automobiles.

Due to the shortage of butter, oleo margarine was introduced. At that time, it was sold in a soft white consistency encased in plastic, with a blister in the center containing an orange substance. It was necessary to break the blister and knead this into the block until it became solid yellow. That was a chore I did not like and, to me, oleo margarine was tasteless. Soybeans were also introduced as a replacement for peanuts.

Many of the neighbors planted victory gardens. My father had spent a number of years living on a farm when he was young and he loved working the soil. He converted half of our backyard into such a garden. He grew tomatoes, peas, green beans, carrots, radishes, beets, squash, spinach, and lettuce, so we always had lots of fresh vegetables in the summertime. Mother preserved and canned many of the items. People who did not have back yards planted gardens in part of the fields behind Dorel Street.

There was a great sadness felt when the death of President Roosevelt was announced as, for many of us, he was the only president we had known in our lifetime. Harry Truman, the vice president, became the new president.

V-E Day (Victory in Europe) and V-J Day (Victory in Japan) were very exciting times in Philadelphia. All businesses closed, and the streets were full of happy people. We knew the war would soon be over and the troops would be coming home once again---this time everyone hoped for good.

After the war, the troops came home. Money began to flow, credit became available, and jobs were plentiful. People began to purchase homes and fix them up. Many enclosed the open front porches with brick or stone fascia, or asbestos shingles. Awnings appeared on the windows to keep out the blistering sun. Combination storm sash and screens were also installed on the windows and doors.

Development flourished. Shopping malls were built. Businesses and industry moved to the outlying suburban areas which had not previously been developed. Housing developments cropped up everywhere. When the service personnel returned home many marriages took place. The young people, and those who could afford it, moved from the city to the suburban and outlying areas. Some moved across the Delaware River to New Jersey where development was also burgeoning, and one could purchase a single home inexpensively. Many of the returning veterans returned to school to finish their education, or to pursue additional training, knowledge, and skills. Their schooling was covered under the G.I. Bill of Rights, which they certainly had earned.

It became customary for young couples to entertain their friends in their homes as an inexpensive way to have a social life. Often times on Friday and Saturday evenings they would roll up the carpets in their living rooms to provide an area for dancing.

Many women also opened their homes and invited friends in to enjoy a pleasant evening of shopping and fun with parties featuring Tupperware, jewelry, cosmetics, and lingerie.

The mid-1940s was a particularly exciting time to be a teenager and living in Philadelphia. It was the era of the *950 Club*, the bobbysoxers, poodle skirts, jukeboxes, jitterbugs.....and, oh yes.....Frank Sinatra came to town. What a thrill that was! *American Bandstand* also arrived on the scene with the loveable Dick Clark as its host.

Hoagie shops and Philly steak sandwich shops were opened and provided a great place for teenagers to hang out. One of our favorite places to go was the *Kozy Korner* on 70th Street, between Elmwood and Buist Avenues. Coca Cola was the "in" drink at that time and was often accompanied by a liverwurst with onion sandwich on rye bread, and a Jewish pickle. Many fun, carefree hours were spent there developing lasting friendships and listening to the favorite hits of the day on the jukebox. I am still in touch and communicate with some of my friends from that era.

The Hot Shoppe in the 69th Street area was also a favorite place to go following a movie, skating, and/or dancing at Chez Vous. They had a drive-in so you could sit in your car and get service, which was novel and very convenient.

Mrs. Scherer, our junior high physical ed teacher, and her husband owned a restaurant on Baltimore Pike in Media, near the Wawa dairy farm, called *Chicken in the Basket.* Their specialty was fried chicken and shoestring potatoes served in a basket. Mrs. Scherer was petite, perky, and very gracious, and always greeted us with a warm hug. That was a fabulous and friendly place to go to eat.

Other favorite hangouts were *Henning's* hoagie shop on Elmwood Avenue, *Tony's* on Woodland Avenue, *Bass's* drugstore at the corner of 67th and Elmwood, and we can't forget *Jaffe's* special shop just a few doors down on Elmwood Avenue. It was incomparable.

Mr. and Mrs. Jaffe operated a small store about ten or twelve feet wide by approximately fifteen feet long. As I recall, the store contained two or three booths, a pinball machine, a telephone booth, a soda fountain, and a display case filled with all kinds of penny candy. You could buy anything you wanted in that little store---candy, cigarettes, soda, pretzels, potato chips, aspirin, newspapers, magazines, etc. You name it, they had it!

At Christmas time many of the people in the neighborhood mentioned special items they wanted to buy. Mr. and Mrs. Jaffe were very congenial people and they obtained these items for them. They also stored toys and games, and many other things for anyone who asked. Nothing was too much trouble for them where friends and neighbors were concerned. They treated us and made us believe that our problems were always their problems, too!

Their son, Allan, was in my class from kindergarten all through high school. Allan was gifted with a great personality and a wonderful sense of humor. Our yearbook described him as "Jack Benny's double." Obviously, he inherited his dad's great personality and both of his parents' sense of caring for others.

Rube Jaffe served the best milk shakes in town, and also offered double dip ice cream cones with chocolate jimmies, or sprinkles, spread all over the top for only five cents. Some cones were called "twin" cones as the dips of ice cream were scooped into cups side by side. At one time, they even served a "triple" side by side cone. That was a challenge to handle! To this day, my husband frequently says he would like to have a "Jaffe's milk shake." They were truly the best around and incomparable!

It was a fun place to go to enjoy a coke and peanut butter squares, or a plate of ice cream and pretzels, and to just listen to our favorite songs on the jukebox while visiting with friends. In addition to being a favorite hangout for teenagers, the men in the neighborhood also congregated there at the end of the workday and on weekends to unwind and enjoy plain old fashioned "guy" talk with other men from the neighborhood, or to just play the pinball machine.

I met my husband at Jaffe's little store. Charlie walked into the store one evening and Mr. Jaffe handed him a nickel and my phone number, and told him he had told me to expect a phone call. My husband has been known to say: "I went in to Jaf's to get a dish of ice cream, was minding my own business, and ended up getting a wife." Thanks, Rube. We've been married over fifty-eight years and we're still together and happy. Among other things, you were a great matchmaker!

Part III
Remembrances of my Family and Family Reunions

I hope this glimpse into the past will be meaningful for the readers. To some, the times may have seemed "tough," but we—families and neighbors alike—were all in the same situation. We didn't complain. We survived! We pulled together and made the most of what we had. We grew from these experiences and we were HAPPY and PRODUCTIVE people. We were taught ethics and respect for others. Instead of expecting to receive from others, we learned to reach out and help whenever and wherever we could to make a difference in the lives of others, which in turn enriched our own lives.

If each of us would try each day to make our corner of the world a better place, the trend may catch on and spread throughout the country and the world. One by one we can make a difference.

Our parents, like many others at that time, were not demonstrative, but we knew we were loved. Hugs and kisses were scarce. They were given more as an obligation rather than a spontaneous act of love. Reaching back into the past has been a delightful experience for me. One memory has led to another, and there are so many more things about which I could write. I have been truly blessed and can sincerely tell you that **"my cup indeed is overflowing."**

Chapter 13
My Family

Now that I have introduced you to the era, the area, and the lifestyle we enjoyed, I would like to introduce you to my immediate and extended family, as they are all an integral part of this memoir, and definitely had a role in making me who I am today.

First, I will disclose what is known about my father's family. We did not know them well nor did we know very much about them during our formative years. They lived at a distance and visits were few and far between because of the distance and other limiting circumstances of the time.

Second, I will disclose what is known about my mother's family. Unlike dad's family, they lived in close proximity to us and we took advantage of the many opportunities for get-togethers.

Third, information about our family reunions is also included, because they were very important gatherings and created many wonderful and lasting memories for us.

MY DAD'S FAMILY

My dad was born in Malvern, Pennsylvania, the fourth of eight children (two boys and six girls). Sometime after his birth in 1899, the family moved from Malvern to a farm in Schwenksville, Pennsylvania.

It is my understanding that his father, Chris, was a building contractor (specializing in carpentry), but, due to a fall from a rooftop, his injuries required a change of occupation. He then became a farmer. In 1914, he was working in the field when an ambulance or fire truck went by. The siren frightened a horse, which knocked him down and trampled him. As a result, his appendix ruptured and he developed peritonitis and died.

The family then moved to West Philadelphia (around 53rd and Media Streets). My grandmother, Mary Jane, ran a boarding house and baked pies which were sold to support the family.

This has not been confirmed, but it is believed that the family stayed in that neighborhood---perhaps the same house---until August 1923. Three of the siblings had married and the fourth, a daughter, was engaged to be married to a boarder who either lived at their house, or at a neighboring house, while the groom-to-be completed his studies at the Philadelphia College of Pharmacology.

When they married, this couple bought a house on North Ardsley Road in Upper Darby, Pennsylvania, near 69th and Market Streets, which was the hub of that area. As previously mentioned, many busses, trolleys, and elevated trains began and terminated their runs at that intersection.

That left our grandmother and the four younger daughters, ages eight, eleven, sixteen, and seventeen, to live with this couple in their home. In 1925, the seventeen-year-old ran away and eloped.

Houses on North Ardsley Road were two-story, one bath, twin houses, and had large living rooms with a stone fireplace, nice size dining room, kitchen, and three bedrooms. The master bedroom was located at the front of the house on the second floor and opened to a lovely sun parlor. There was a drive behind the house and a garage with an entrance from the rear, and a basement.

Because of time and circumstances, we only visited them about once a year until grandmother had a stroke in 1946 and was confined to bed. Generally, grandmother came to visit us and had dinner with us around her birthday (June 21) and on Thanksgiving. She customarily left immediately after Thanksgiving to spend the winter in Lakeland, Florida, where she visited with one of her daughters and her family.

Grandmother was a very soft-spoken, sweet lady who loved to crochet. She made each of her granddaughters a little crocheted purse and white gloves, which were very stylish at that time. I still have the bedspread/tablecloth that she made while in her late seventies. She was ill for three years and, on her deathbed, she told me she wished things had been different, and that she could have spent more time with all of her grandchildren. Time and circumstances did not provide the opportunity for her to get to know them as well as she would have liked. That comment stayed with me and encouraged me to be certain to devote quality time with my grandchildren when I became a grandmother.

It is believed that grandmother had several brothers, but the only sibling I recall ever meeting was an uncle, Evan, who married the daughter of the owner of the Kerr Paper Mill in Downingtown, Pennsylvania. They were a delightful couple who lived in a three-story twin home on Lincoln Highway, aka Lancaster Pike. (They owned both of the twin homes and a granddaughter lived in the home adjoining theirs on the other side.) The home had a large backyard, and there was a either a Model A or Model T Ford parked in the garage at the rear of the property.

Uncle Evan worked at the paper mill and I can recall when he turned eighty, he told my dad that he was cutting down and wasn't going to work seven days a week anymore because it was getting to be too much. He said he was only going to work six days. He enjoyed listening to the radio and never missed listening to the Philadelphia A's and Phillies baseball games. Uncle Evan died in the early 1960s.

Aunt Katie was a very sweet, little, white-haired lady who was totally deaf. She sat in a chair and smiled constantly. She seemed to enjoy having company come to visit even though she was hearing impaired. Aunt Katie died in 1958.

They had one son and two daughters who all lived in town, and we visited with them and their families also when we went to Downingtown. My dad loved this aunt and uncle and always enjoyed going to visit them. He spent many summers with them when he was growing up, and he treasured the memories and frequently spoke of them.

Dad talked about several of his uncles, including one named Atmore, but we never met them. His family had a number of relatives (including a cousin who was a justice of the peace) who lived in Juniata County, in western Pennsylvania. Unfortunately, I don't know much about dad's oldest sister, Viola. She and her husband, Crawford, an accountant, lived in Norristown, Pennsylvania, and later moved to Jeffersonville, Pennsylvania. This to us was the other end of the world because it took over an hour to drive there. Occasionally we would take a drive to visit them, or they would take a bus into the city to see us. At times we would meet at the family home in Upper Darby, but they were very rare occasions. Aunt Viola died in 1943 following a lengthy illness. I have been told that she was a very caring and thoughtful person, and, when she was well and times were tough, she made certain we all had gifts to open at Christmastime.

They raised one son, Crawford, who served in the Army during World War II. He graduated from Duke. Later he owned a paint and lacquer company in Tampa, Florida. As an adult I met him on several occasions. We exchanged notes, cards, and occasional telephone calls. He was married and raised four children---two boys and two girls. His first wife, Ginny, his college sweetheart, died in 1984. He then married a lovely widow, Anne, who also had four children. They enjoyed travelling until his death in January 2004.

Dad's only brother, Clarence, and his wife, Mae, lived on a farm (about 100 acres) in Faggs Manor, later known as Cochranville, Pennsylvania. Uncle Clarence farmed the land until World War II. At that time, he left to work at Lukens Steel Mill in Coatesville. He was a mill operator, inspector, and later a supervisor. He was a mild, slender man, and always appeared to be in very good health. I recall hearing that one morning he got up, dressed, and went downstairs for breakfast, sat at the table, and died. He was eighty-two years of age and had not been ill. He died in January 1977.

His wife, Aunt Mae, studied to be a school teacher and was very articulate, and had beautiful penmanship. She had a very sharp mind and communicated with me by letters until shortly before her death. She loved her home which was cited as a historic place because it was situated on the Brandywine

Battlefield, and was over 100 years old. Aunt Mae took great pride in her home and had it completely modernized. Her hobby was cultivating African violets and she had a beautiful collection of them. Aunt Mae died in November 1990.

Together they raised a son, Harold, and four daughters, Betty, Jane, Dorothy, and Nancy; and it was always fun to go and visit them. We, being city kids, enjoyed seeing the animals when they farmed the land, and loved romping through the acreage of open fields.

The next aunt and uncle was an interesting couple. Aunt Bert was a very reserved, serious person with very strong likes and dislikes, and Uncle Ernest was a comic---a laugh a minute. [Example: he would tell stories about my grandmother painting her toenails bright red so that when she got up in the middle of the night she could see without putting on a light. He also told us she had a boyfriend whom he always referred to as "Peg-leg Pete." Supposedly, Grandmother was engaged to marry this individual. Both of these stories were completely made-up.] He was sure a wild storyteller and loved teasing people. Everyone just laughed at his antics.

Prior to their marriage, Aunt Bert worked as a bookkeeper/statistician for the Curtis Publishing Company in Philadelphia, Pennsylvania. Uncle Ernest was a pharmacist and worked at a drugstore in the vicinity of 69th Street and Marshall Road, Upper Darby, Pennsylvania, and later in Hollywood, Florida.

If any of the family visited the drugstore when he was working, he made certain they were treated to ice cream or sodas of some sort. That was in the days when drugstores had soda fountains and people who worked at the soda fountain were called "soda jerks." They both liked ice cream and Breyers was always the favorite brand served at their home.

Uncle Ernest loved sports and kept abreast of high school and college activities, as well as the major leagues. He could converse with anyone on any subject. He served in France in the Army during World War I, and was gassed. Uncle Ernest was a very compassionate man, and he and Aunt Bert helped to raise the two youngest sisters. They enrolled them both in Pierce Business School in Philadelphia, so they could learn business skills. They had no children of their own. They moved to Miami, Florida in the early 1950s. Uncle Ernest died in 1974, and Aunt Bert died in 1983.

My dad came next in line and he was a very warm and compassionate man. He was named for his dad, but he did not like the first name and dropped it in later life. After that, he went only by his middle name, which was Albert. Dad was slated to attend Williamson Trade School in Media, Pennsylvania, to learn the building trade, but the death of his father when he was fourteen altered the plans. Dad had to leave school and he went to work at a ball bearing plant to help support the family.

He later went to work at the General Electric Company Switchgear Plant in Southwest Philadelphia as a machine operator, and advanced to foreman. He was also a shop steward. After thirty-two years of service, he had to retire in December 1956, due to ill health. He had four heart conditions as the result of having had rheumatic fever as a young child.

Dad was active in church work and served on the administrative board and was an active member of the men's group at the Clearview Methodist Church, 76th Street and Buist Avenue. He also enjoyed doing various jobs modernizing the house---carpentry, painting, tiling, wall papering, gardening etc. He also loved children, and he was loved by all. There were many times that he didn't have much, but he gave what he could and taught us to do the same. He was an extremely generous person.

He married my mother, Sylvania, a descendant of the Penn family, in October 1922. Mother came from a family of ten children---five boys and five girls. Her parents separated when the children were young, and three of them lived with the father and the others lived with the mother who reportedly was ill. The older siblings assumed all of the household responsibilities, as well as helping to raise the younger children while, at the same time, holding outside jobs. Together mother and dad raised six children---three girls and three boys: Mildred, Walter, Violet, James, Ruth, and Bob.

Aunt Margaret followed my dad in the birth order. She married Uncle John, who was a wrestler and postmaster of Cheswold, Delaware, where they made their home. We rarely saw them because of time and distance. Occasionally we would meet at the relatives' home in Upper Darby. I recall hearing that in earlier days, they often got together with a group including my parents to play cards. They also camped out frequently at a place called "Green Lane."

Aunt Margaret was a packer in a candy factory. She had a brain aneurysm, was hospitalized, and spent her final days in a nursing home, prior to her death in the early 1960s.

Uncle John was a boxer, and in addition to being postmaster at Cheswold, Delaware, he was also the fire chief. It was at a banquet in his honor that he succumbed to a heart attack in September 1956.

Aunt Margaret and Uncle John had one son, John Jr., who was called Junior. He was married and had three daughters. Junior served in the Navy during World War II. His first wife, Bonnie, died in 1968, and he remarried. He won $100,000 in a state lottery, and died in November 1982.

Aunt Mabel, who married Uncle Joe, followed next in the birth order. They lived most of their lives in Lakeland, Florida. For a year or so they lived on Timberlake Road in Upper Darby, Pennsylvania, and we were able to get acquainted with them since we did exchange visits with them on a number of occasions. Those visits were fun.

Aunt Mabel was a very sweet, soft-spoken lady who, like the youngest sister, was most like our grandmother in disposition and appearance. She married young and had a very difficult life, but remained strong in her faith, her love of God, and her family. She was an excellent cook and hostess, and was a dietician at Lakeland Memorial Hospital.

Uncle Joe, her husband, was an independent plumber. He had been injured in the military in World War I and had a metal plate in his head. My dad always said of him: "You couldn't meet a nicer man than Joe ." He and Aunt Mabel had a son who died in childhood, and two daughters---Anne and Pat. Anne's husband, Carl, worked with Uncle Joe in the plumbing business. They had four children. Pat was married to a former judge of Dade City, Florida. They had three children in addition to the two she had from a previous marriage. Aunt Mae and Uncle Joe divorced in the 1950s. Uncle Joe remarried and died several years later. Aunt Mabel died in October 1979.

Aunt Dot was born next to the youngest. She never married. A graduate from Pierce Business School in Philadelphia, Pennsylvania, she was employed as the secretary to the sales manager at Foss Hughes, a large Ford motor dealership in downtown Philadelphia. She worked there until her move to Florida in 1952.

Aunt Dot was a very stylish dresser and could be a lot of fun. She was active in her church in Florida, and enjoyed doing canvas needlepoint. One Easter she made 100 crosses that were given to those who attended church that day. She worked as a waitress until she broke her leg in an accident. After her recovery she took care of the housekeeping chores and tended to her sister, Aunt Bert, until her death in 1983. Aunt Dot later moved to Lakeland where she lived until her death in January 2004.

Aunt Marie was the youngest of the eight children. She was very petite, soft spoken, and just as sweet as they come. She reminded me very much of our grandmother. Her husband, Uncle Ted, was very tall and slender, and a very compassionate man. They seemed to be a perfect match, and I always called them the "bookends." They were a fun and very loving couple, and it was always a joy to visit with them.

Uncle Ted was an accountant who worked for Mackle Brothers, a land developer in the Miami area. He enjoyed making hook rugs and doing needlepoint on canvas. Together they enjoyed playing cards and they were active in the Methodist Church and the senior citizens group at the church, and later at the retirement home where they spent their last days. They had one son who only lived fifteen hours, and a second son who is an attorney; and one grandson. Aunt Marie died in 1980; Uncle Ted died in September 1997.

MY MOTHER'S FAMILY

Things were different with mother's family. When we were growing up eight of the ten siblings lived within a two square-mile area---the same area in which they were born and raised. As a result, we got together with these aunts, uncles, and cousins frequently and met them at various functions at school, church, and shopping, so we knew them quite well. They were very much a part of our daily lives.

My maternal grandmother was the daughter of Emma Penn. Her daughter, my grandmother, was born in September 1860 and died in July 1924, so I never had the opportunity to meet her, nor have I ever seen pictures of her as an adult. It is my understanding that she attended normal school and was educated to be a school teacher.

She married my grandfather, William, at the Broad Street M.E. Church on November 17, 1887. Even though they began married life in a three-story house in downtown Philadelphia, we were always told the family felt she married beneath their standards. It is reported that their house was completely furnished and had luxury items such as gold-framed mirrors, plush carpets, and a piano. Although ten children were born to this marriage, it reportedly was not a happy marriage and the couple was estranged for many years. Some of the children lived with the mother and several lived with the father. The older children had to leave school early and seek employment to assist in supporting the family.

My grandfather was born in 1860 and died in May 1939. He was employed at times as a butcher, a stoker, and, in his later years, he worked at an ice house which was located by the trolley barn near Island Road and Elmwood Avenue. My oldest sister, who is seven years older than me, has told me that our father sent her on secret missions to visit him at the ice house on several occasions due to our dad's compassion and concern for him. Dad wanted to be sure he was doing okay. Grandfather was estranged from some of his family.

The only recollection I have of my maternal Grandfather occurred when I was about four years of age. He was living with Aunt Em up the street, and, one day when I was staying with Aunt Em, he gave me a party favor which was popular at that particular time—a figure made out of toothpicks and various colored gumdrops. Aunt Em was horrified and immediately took it away from me because her dog had chewed on it. Apparently it did not bother me. I was thrilled to know that I had a grandfather since I had never heard anything about him, and, to my knowledge, I never saw him again, nor was he ever mentioned. In those days family secrets were never discussed, and one is left to draw their own conclusions since it was not customary for children to raise questions as they do today. Many people felt that "children should be seen and not heard," and we heard that phrase frequently.

Aunt Emma was the oldest of the ten children born to this marriage. She was the epitome of a homemaker, and she loved every aspect of it. I can still envision her working in her large kitchen wearing a freshly starched apron, standing at the ironing board carefully ironing and folding every piece of laundry that she had lovingly laundered. She even ironed socks, tea towels, terry towels, etc., which most women didn't have time to do and would never even consider doing.

At the same time Aunt Em was ironing, she was preparing a feast for the evening meal. She always served a full-course dinner, including a roast of some sort, salad, potatoes, gravy, fresh vegetables, homemade rolls or biscuits, and dessert. It was fun watching her beat egg whites to perfection to top off a lemon meringue pie which was baking in the oven. She was truly a multi-tasker, took great pride in everything she did, and it was done meticulously.

My sister told me that she often watched as Aunt Em patiently and carefully hung her laundry in a very painstaking fashion. She prided herself in copying Aunt Em's style when she became a homemaker and it was her turn to hang laundry outside on the line.

In those days, in that area (circa 1930-1940), it was acceptable to "drop in" for a visit without an invitation, and family, friends and neighbors all took advantage of that.

Visitors were always warmly received at Aunt Em's, but it was understood that she would continue with her chores while one visited with her. She was a very compassionate woman who truly cared about everyone, whether she knew them or not.

Two of my nephews, Marshall and Philip, were raised in the South. Their father, who had been raised in the Atlanta, Georgia area, died as the result of polio when Marshall was three years of age and Philip just thirteen months old. Their mother wanted them to be raised in that same area so they could know their paternal relatives and also the land in which their father had been raised. Shortly after arriving for their annual visit to Philadelphia, the duo excitedly asked if they could run up the street to see Aunt Emma. They said they knew her house because "it had an 'M' on the door for Emma." Hearing that story always tickled her and she loved hearing it and repeating it to everyone each year.

Aunt Em loved to shop and never missed a Strawbridge & Clothier "Clover Day" or Gimbel Brothers "Founder's Day," as on those special days both stores had great sales. She had gifts stored in her bedroom available to be wrapped and delivered for any occasion that should arise...be it a birthday, new baby, wedding, etc. She was a very stylish dresser, and dressed to the nines whenever she went out.

Aunt Em belonged to the Siloam Methodist Church for over fifty years, and was also a member of the Philathea Sunday school class, which she attended faithfully until her death in 1965.

Aunt Em married Uncle Bert, a widower with two young daughters, Ruby and Ellen. He was a stone mason and, along with two other uncles, worked on the construction of the Philadelphia Art Museum. Uncle Bert was a large man who wore blue denim overalls, He appeared to be rather gruff, and, as kids, we were afraid of him. Later in life, I learned that he was a very tender and caring man. He earned a living buying houses and remodeling them for either sale or rental purposes. He always drove a Studebaker. No other car would do.

Aunt Em and Uncle Bert had two children: a son, Irvin, who served in the Army during World War II, and was the ring bearer in my parents' wedding, and a daughter, Kathryn, who retired from the Bell Telephone Company following a lifelong career. Irv married Obby, an elementary school teacher, and they had three children: Betty Jean, Bertram, and Kathy, all of whom teach school. Irv and his son, Bertram, also had an automobile supply store in Wheaton, Maryland until Irv retired. He died in 2005.

Their daughter, Kathryn, was married twice. Her first husband, Glenn, served in the U.S. Navy during World War II. He died in 1965. She then married George. She had no children and died in 1983.

Aunt Em and Uncle Bert had a large police dog named Vonnie, who was crippled and jealous of children. When visitors called, Vonnie would position herself between two rooms, or at the top of the stairway, to make passing a challenge. When Vonnie died, the family adopted a black-and-white spotted springer named "Penny." Penny was full of energy and constantly jumped on people.

Aunt Em and her family lived up the street from us, and we saw them daily. Their home was the gathering place when cousins and other out-of-town relatives came to the area to visit. Aunt Em frequently visited us also, and we lovingly called her the "bearer of glad tidings," since she was well informed on the latest matters pertaining to family, friends, and neighbors.

They had a summer home in Chester Heights, Pennsylvania, outside of Philadelphia, in a community of the Methodist church campgrounds and meetings. A number of people had homes or cottages at Chester Heights and would go out there to spend the summer to escape the heat of the city, as houses were not air conditioned at that time. The summer homes at Chester Heights were bungalows or cottages and did not have indoor plumbing. Aunt Em and Uncle Bert's house was a two-story, white frame house with red trim, and had both running water and electricity. Due to Uncle Bert's many skills, it was more modern than most of the homes in the area.

Aunt Em took me out there several times to spend a week or more with her to keep her company during the summer. Sometimes another cousin would also be there, so there was someone with whom to play. We roamed the campgrounds, played on the playground equipment, and visited with the people in the area, and I'm sure we probably were a big nuisance to the neighbors.

When Uncle Bert died in June 1946, Aunt Em took in boarders who worked at a local defense plant. It provided her with a source of income and also companionship. They filled a void in her life and she was very good to them and treated them as family. Aunt Em died in May 1965.

Next in line was Aunt Florence, who we called "Aunt Floss" or just plain "Aunt," and she was truly one of a kind! She never married and, since she attended the same church that we did, we saw her frequently so we knew her quite well.

On Sundays after church, we took her to our home for lunch. She always wore a hat and coat and would not remove them regardless of the temperature, and summertime in Philadelphia can be a scorcher---particularly since the homes were not air-conditioned back then. Her famous comment when asked if we could take her coat was: "I don't know how long I'm staying." Of course, she was always still there when it was time for dinner and to go to church in the evening.

This may not be totally accurate, but, from what I understand, several of the siblings put together to buy the house she lived in, and, as they married, she bought their share so she ended up with the house. It was a large house with large rooms. In later years, the upstairs was converted into an apartment.

When the siblings all married and left, Aunt Floss took in boarders, which was the "in" thing to do in those days. This was during the Depression and pre-World War II era, and money and jobs were scarce. People did whatever they could to get the money needed to make ends meet and to survive.

One such boarder was seen by us, as kids, to be a persnickety elderly woman named Gertrude. She was always fastidiously dressed in black, and wore a string of pearls around her neck, and, in reality, she was probably a lovely woman whom we had misjudged. Her beautiful white hair was always carefully coiffed and she never had a single strand out of place. Miss Gertrude disliked children and was not a happy camper anytime children visited. We had the run of the house when we were visiting Aunt Floss so I'm sure we contributed to her portrayal of unhappiness.

Two other women whom I remember living there at Aunt Floss's house were Miss Norman, who had lived next door with her mother and moved in with Aunt Floss when her mother died, and Mrs. Brady. Both were seemingly very elderly women from England. They wore long flowing dresses with long sleeves and high necklines, and high-top shoes. Both Miss Norman and Mrs. Brady were very friendly and treated us children very kindly.

When I was about four or five years of age, I remember that Aunt Floss took me to visit the "home for the blind," which was located somewhere around 68th Street and Woodland Avenue. I could not understand why the rooms were always dark and no one ever turned on any of the lights. The people seemed to me to be very old, but were all very kind. They all had glass jars containing assorted hard candy which they graciously offered to us.

Another place Aunt Floss took me to visit was commonly referred to as an "old folks" home up in the Germantown area. It was a long trip by public transportation. I recall these visits as being rather uncomfortable and frightening experiences for me as a young child.

At the time I was too young to know and understand that Aunt Floss was performing a ministry. She was also teaching me, by example, to care about others. We all have the awesome responsibility to reach out to others and spread God's love, and to try to make a difference in someone else's life. This was truly an example of living by the "golden rule."

In addition to children, Aunt Floss loved cats. At one time she had as many as thirty-two cats of different sizes, colors, and varieties. She bought them fresh milk, and cooked fish and chicken livers for them. The front cellar window was always kept open to provide an entrance and exit for them to come and go as they pleased. When the neighbors reported her to the board of health and they came to investigate, she convinced the authorities that she treated her cats better than they treated their children, so no action was ever taken.

Aunt Floss also had an old mean, green parrot that screeched constantly when anyone visited. The story we were told was that a man, who knew and befriended one of our uncles, had skipped ship and brought the bird with him. When he got caught, he had to leave the country. He asked one of our uncles to care for the bird until he returned. The man never returned and the bird became a real nuisance. Aunt Floss volunteered to take the bird and care for it, and she did care for it very lovingly until it died on Christmas Eve 1950.

A cousin recently told me that she and another cousin were told that the reason Aunt Floss took the bird was because someone told her the bird sang hymns. Try as they could, they could never get the bird to sing. It only screeched! Kids being kids, we always teased the bird by saying: "Polly, wanna cracker?" That made the parrot screech even louder.

There is a cemetery at the corner of the street where Aunt Floss lived. Our grandparents and some of our aunts, uncles, and cousins are buried there. Yes, you guessed it! Polly is also buried there along with many of the cats, since Aunt Floss wanted to have them all buried with her. When one of the pets died, as youngsters, it was our job to take the wagon over to Aunt Floss's house, place the carefully wrapped pet into the wagon, and deliver it to the cemetery for burial. We received a dime for our services each time we performed this deed. That was a big deal for us! It made us feel very important.

Visiting Aunt Floss was always a fun experience. Her enclosed porch led to an entryway, which must have been six or seven feet square, with two sets of double doors. One set opened to the porch and the second set opened to a hallway. This vestibule provided us with many hours of pleasure as it was the perfect place to play "elevator." Aunt Floss had a rotating piano stool which we were permitted to use. The elevator operator sat on the stool, and it was great to give the passenger the illusion of going up and down. Sometimes, because we were taught to share fairly, the passenger also had a turn to sit on the stool.

We often visited Aunt Floss on Saturdays and stayed for dinner. When Aunt Floss asked if we were going to stay for dinner we, in unison, said: "Our mother said we could only stay for dinner if we were invited." Of course we stayed, and Aunt Floss prepared whatever we asked for. One sister liked potato salad so she made potato salad. Another liked macaroni and cheese and cottage cheese, so they were added to the menu. Whatever we asked for, she prepared. Nothing was too much trouble for her when we visited.

We would follow her to the basement (cellar), which seemed like a dungeon to us as it was large and very dark. The only light was a single light bulb extending from the ceiling on a long black cord. We were permitted to select cans of vegetables and whatever else we thought we wanted to eat. If Aunt Floss didn't have the desired foods in the house, she would take us to the corner grocery store and buy it, plus anything else we saw that we thought we wanted.

Aunt Floss involved us in a number of interesting activities which included "digging a tunnel to China" in the backyard. Our father did not appreciate that activity and discouraged it because it left big holes in the carefully tended yard. She also taught us to "catch Japanese beetles in a jar," and the one who caught the most was promised a trip to Japan (which never happened). We also spent time "catching fireflies, aka lightning bugs."

One sister recently told me she remembers climbing to the ceiling on the water pipes in the dining room. That was before my day so I have no firsthand knowledge of it, but, from other stories I have heard, I'm sure it happened.

If we became unruly, Aunt Floss's favorite saying was: "I'll sit on your neck and break it." I guess we weren't too bad because I don't recall any of us ever having a broken neck.

She always wore her long dark hair pulled straight back and in a bun, secured by hairpins. Her hair was so long she could sit on it. Never would she permit anyone to cut it.

Aunt Floss worked at the Frankford Arsenal during World War II. We never knew anything about her job, but she promised when she retired, she would buy a motor home and take all her nieces and nephews on a tour of the United States. She did retire, but the trip never happened!

After World War II, she worked at a company that made cake decorations. As we married, she gave each one of us the "bride and groom" ornament for the top tier of our wedding cake.

My siblings and I have concluded that every family should be fortunate enough to be blessed with an aunt like Aunt Floss. She sure made our lives interesting and provided us with many wonderful memories and laughs! I'm sure that, in return, we kept her life from being uneventful and boring, too. Aunt Floss died in February 1973.

Uncle Bill was next in the birth order. He married a lady name Ethel, who was born in England. As kids we did not know them because time and circumstances did not provide the opportunity to visit back and forth, as they lived across the river in New Jersey. We did meet on several occasions at family gatherings later in the early 1950s. They were very pleasant people. As I recall, Aunt Ethel was petite, very sweet, and soft-spoken, and had beautiful red hair.

Uncle Bill died in March 1966. Aunt Ethel died in January 1971.

They raised two daughters with whom I have communicated and also exchanged email messages. One daughter, Wilda, lived in Medford, New Jersey, until her death in May 2009. She was the flower girl in my parents' wedding. The other daughter, Emma, lives in Virginia Beach, Virginia, and I remain in regular contact with her.

Aunt Katherine, called "Katie," was next in line. She married Uncle Win, and they raised two sons, Winfield and Wilfred. Winfield served in the Army during World War II, and retired from E.I.duPont, where he worked as a metallurgist. His wife, Joan, has died. They had two children: a son and a daughter. Wilfred retired from Curtis Publishing Company and died in 1994. Uncle Win was a metallurgist and worked at Piasecki Helicopter plant. He died in 1962.

It was always fun to visit Aunt Katie. No matter what she was doing when someone visited, unlike Aunt Emma, she would stop to sit and chat. I think she and her neighbors invented the "koffee klatch." Having her nieces visit brought her great joy since she was raising two sons, and the girls provided an interesting change of pace for her and diverse topics of conversation, in which boys wouldn't engage.

Aunt Katie also enjoyed cooking. I remember having dinner at their home one evening and there were two main entrees: one son wanted ham and the other one wanted roast beef, so she prepared both.

Mother was ill when I was small and I spent a number of days and nights at Aunt Katie's house. The boys always enjoyed teasing me since I was a girl and they were older.

In their later years, the five sisters started a "sewing circle" and used to gather for lunch and stitching at each other's homes. They seemed to enjoy the time they spent together as adults, after their families were raised and their spouses began dying. This gathering provided an outlet that filled a void in their lives. It was a fun pastime for them and it was a good opportunity for them to relax and enjoy their sisterhood.

Aunt Katie died in November 1982.

Uncle Al was next in line and was married to Aunt Elizabeth. He was a 'huckster'. As I stated earlier, in those days there were a few small mom-and-pop grocery stores on various corners, but the large food markets were few and far between. The big grocery shopping had to be done by automobile or public transportation, and usually occurred on Friday nights or Saturdays. If you didn't have an automobile, groceries were carted home in a wagon. During the week, hucksters walked up and down the back alleys behind the row houses with baskets of fresh fruit and produce, and offered them for sale to the residents. Uncle Al gave us tangerines and seasonal items when we saw him. It made us feel special, and we always looked forward to seeing him.

Uncle Al and Aunt Elizabeth had five daughters: Elizabeth, Ruth, Frances, Esther, and Doris. All are still living with the exception of Esther, who died in 2002.

Uncle Al died in December 1985. Aunt Elizabeth died in October 1977.

Aunt Edith came next. She was married to Uncle Abner and they raised two sons: Abner Jr. and John. Uncle Abner was a wallpaper hanger and played the mandolin as a hobby. He died in January 1957.

Aunt Edith was known for making braided rugs and was an avid coordinator for the "blanket club." She paid me twenty-five cents a week to go around and collect twenty-five cent dues from the members. When their contributions reached $6.25, they could select a blanket. It was a means to "buy merchandise on time," and the participants seemed to enjoy the activity.

During World War II, she, like many other women, worked at the local defense plant, but I have no idea what she did. The family moved to Dorothy, New Jersey after World War II because Uncle Abner was not well, and it was felt the climate at the New Jersey shore would be better for his health. Aunt Edith then worked for the Ocean Spray Cranberry Company. She loved sewing and gardening; and grew fresh vegetables which she preserved. She died in May 1990.

Young Abner used to ride a two-wheel bicycle when he came to visit. He used to take us for rides on the handlebars. Later, he had a little car with a rumble seat, which was fun to ride in. It was probably a 1929 or early 1930s version. Abner Jr. was also interested in aviation, and, following World War II, he served in the Civil Air Patrol. John served in the Army during World War II.

Young Abner's wife, Beaulah, preceded him in death. They had one son.

John's wife, Mary, also died. They had two sons and a daughter.

Both Abner Jr. and John were highly intelligent young men. They were active in boy scouting and belonged to Troop 277 which met at Karmel Lutheran Church on Elmwood Avenue around 71st or 72nd Street. They were both very mechanical-minded and very handy. They built electric trains from tin cans. They also built their own homes in Dorothy, New Jersey, on the family property, adjacent to their parents' home. Both are deceased, having died in the last decade. I don't have their exact dates.

Uncle Harry was next in line. He married Aunt Mary. They lived in a white frame with green trim two-story twin house, next to Mary's brother and sister-in law. Even though they lived in the neighborhood, we did not see them very often. Uncle Harry was a huckster and also delivered coal for the Mills Company. In those days the homes had coal furnaces for heating, and the trucks delivered coal into the coal bin area of the basements. It was fun for kids to watch the little black lumps of coal slide down the chute and into the window leading to the coal bin.

They had one son and two daughters. Their son died at the age of two years, reportedly the result of a reaction to eating a peach prior to taking a nap. One daughter, Florence, was very active in the church and community in Surf City, New Jersey, where she lived with her second husband, Frank. Florence loved to do crafts, needlepoint, and crocheting. She is now deceased. It is believed that the second daughter, Marion, lives in Delaware County, Pennsylvania. We never got to know her, and, to my knowledge, she has not been in contact with any other members of the family either.

Uncle Harry died in March 1975. Aunt Mary died in April 1981.

My mother, Sylvania, was the eighth born of the ten children. I've been told that according to tradition one male son in the family had to have "Penn" as part of his name; and one female had to have some form of the name "Pennsylvania" in their name. Hence Mother was named "Sylvania." (My oldest sister is named "Mildred Sylvania.") Prior to marrying my father, Albert, mother was an elevator operator and a yarn packer. She enjoyed designing and sewing clothes for herself and for her children. Her sisters told us that she had a knack for seeing an outfit in a fashionable shop, going home, and recreating it. Obviously, that was a talent she probably inherited from her Grandmother Penn who, with her two sisters, was a milliner and had a dressmaking business in Philadelphia. The story has been told that the opening of John Wanamaker's Department Store put them out of business.

Mother had a black molded dress form which she kept in the cellar. The dress form was named "Miriam," and at Halloween, it was brought upstairs and a white sheet was thrown over it to make it look like a ghost. As kids, we were always afraid to go to the cellar because of our fear of this creature called "Miriam." During the Depression, Mother bought material at ten cents a yard and made clothes for all of us.

Mother lived to be almost 102 years of age. She was very active in the Southwest Philadelphia senior citizens center, and taught their Wednesday morning Bible study class. Mother attended night school and earned her high school diploma while in her 70s, and enjoyed doing crafts and painting for hobbies. One of her paintings won an award and was hung in the capitol building in Harrisburg, Pennsylvania when she was 90 years of age. She lived in three centuries, having been born in 1898 and she died in 2000.

She married our father, Albert, in October 1922. Dad was a machinist and worked at the General Electric Company Switchgear Plant in Southwest Philadelphia. He was a shop steward and foreman, and, during World War II, worked seven days a week. His dayshift often extended into the 4:00 p.m. - midnight shift, and he also had to spend time on the graveyard shift frequently to keep production running, so we didn't see too much of him during that period. He retired in December 1956, after thirty-two years of service, due to heart disease. Dad died in December 1961.

Together they raised six children: three boys and three girls---Mildred, Walter, Violet, James, Ruth, and Robert. James and Walter both died in 2008; Bob died in 2009.

Uncle Wilfred was next in line. He was a design engineer and was employed by the General Electric Company, from which he retired. His wife, Catherine (Aunt Kay), was the daughter of a prominent Methodist minister. Aunt Kay worked at the Federal Reserve Bank in downtown Philadelphia, from which she retired. They moved from their home in Lansdowne to Oxford, Pennsylvania, and had planned to raise sheep until Uncle Wilfred took ill and died in 1966. They had no children. Aunt Kay lived in a retirement home in Quarryville until her death in 1985.

Uncle Ted was the youngest of the ten children. He was involved in various business adventures--gas stations, real estate, machine shop, etc. He bought a 200-acre farm on the Brandywine Battlefield at Honeybrook, Pennsylvania, and became a "gentleman farmer." He built a machine shop there and manufactured small parts for neighboring small companies. During World War II, he made bullets for the Dutch Army.

The farm had an old stone farmhouse and had neither water nor electricity. There was an old pump at the back of the house which had to be primed to get their water. Because they did not have an indoor bathroom, there was an outhouse. Of course, Uncle Ted had the house modernized so it was habitable for him and his wife, Aunt Pearl, and he did install an indoor bathroom.

Aunt Pearl made candy favors and decorations for a five and ten cents store in the 69th Street shopping area. She was a lovely woman and everyone adored her. They had only one daughter, Margaret. Several times over the years, before they moved to the farm, I spent a week or two at their home during the summers when they lived in Highland Park, Upper Darby. They were always favorites of the entire family; and they frequently came to the city to visit. Aunt Pearl died in 1970, and Uncle Ted married again. His second wife was Lillian (Lee) Mandarano. Lee died prior to Uncle Ted who died in 2003, in his 100th year of life.

Their daughter, Margaret, has seven children and a number of grandchildren and great-grandchildren. She and her first husband, Bill, had three daughters. She and her second husband, Chuck, had two daughters and two sons.

Chapter 14
Family Reunions

Following the death of my maternal grandfather in 1939, the family decided to hold annual family reunions. Initially, these picnics were held at the Upper Darby Township Park, which was also known as Seven Springs Park and Naylor's Run. It was a lovely park with large picnic areas, swings, slides, and seesaws, which were also known as teeter-totters.

The park had a creek running through it, and signs were posted prohibiting swimming and fishing. I recall vividly the trestle over the creek where trains crossed overhead. What a sight for "city" kids to experience! We were used to seeing trains run at ground and below ground level, and even the els that ran overhead…but we never saw a train run over a creek in a park. That was new and fascinating to us city kids!

The older cousins were "teenagers" and we thought really cool. They taught us to climb up and walk across the trestle tracks. This is a very dangerous and frightening experience for youngsters, and should not be attempted unless accompanied by responsible adults who know the area and the time trains are scheduled to cross.

Crossing the trestle was also exciting because one could look between the boards (railroad ties) and see the creek below. It was also dangerous because children couldn't possibly know the distance from the trestle to the creek should they fall, nor could they know the depth of the water, nor could they know what lived in the creek (fish, snakes, turtles, etc.) It was also mysterious! Rocks, stones, and water were the only visible things the eye could see when looking down from the trestle tracks. Imaginations could run rampant wondering about other possibilities.

The teenage cousins made the experience more interesting and frightening because, as we crossed the tracks, they kept telling us stories about hearing a train approaching and stressing that we needed to hurry across. They constantly made comments about someone losing their balance and falling into the creek. That's one memory I'll never forget!

There also was a stone wall across the creek that we walked on to get to the other side of the park. That was exciting and also scary because if we had fallen, we would have gone right into the water.....and it's anyone's guess what could have happened then!

During World War II, the park was closed for security reasons, which necessitated finding a new location to hold our reunion. Uncle Wilfred and Aunt Kay graciously opened their home in Lansdowne. They lived in a large three-story stone twin home that had an enormous back yard. We gathered there until after the war when development in suburban Philadelphia became rampant. The local school district purchased most of their land to accommodate school growth, making it no longer feasible for large gatherings.

At that time, Uncle Ted and Aunt Pearl were living on an old farm located on the Brandywine Battlefield. The property consisted of 200 acres and had a creek and lots of large rocks and thick woods through which one could roam. It also had a stone farmhouse that was over 100 years old that had neither electricity nor running water. There was an outhouse and water was pumped from a well at the back of the house outside the kitchen door.

After modernizing the house, Uncle Ted built a cinder-block building to house a machine shop, where he made small parts for industrial and farm equipment as well as bullets for the Dutch army.

They invited us to have the picnics at their farm. Everyone enjoyed visiting them and it was an ideal and fun spot for a family reunion and picnic. The gatherings were changed to Labor Day, and it was a fun and relaxing outing that everyone looked forward to attending before beginning the hectic fall schedule.

Each family brought their own picnic lunch, but there was always plenty of fresh corn, tomatoes, etc. from the farm and other goodies which everyone shared. We played quoits (aka horseshoes), badminton, croquet, and romped through the acreage and woods enjoying nature at its best. The children also enjoyed pony rides and romping with the dogs (one was a collie named Bonnie which was from the Lassie lineage), pigs, chickens, goats, horses, and cows.

Most of the grown-ups, who didn't participate in the annual baseball game, were happy to have a day to just relax and visit with each other, catching up on family happenings.

We all have wonderful memories of the farm and the reunions we held there. My family is extremely grateful to our cousin, Margaret, and her family for graciously opening her father's home and the farm to us which enabled us to hold one last reunion there following mother's burial in July 2000. This was the very last time we had an opportunity to visit with Uncle Ted; and also several of our cousins—Irvin, John and Abner. They, Esther and our brothers, all passed on in the last decade. We will be eternally thankful for that experience and the wonderful memories it provided.

Families and family reunions are special and create memories that are precious reminders that cannot be erased!

Epilogue

Many years have passed since those memorable days of the 1930s and 1940s. Events and circumstances have taken my siblings and me to different parts of the country---away from the area in which we were raised and on to new places and new experiences.

Prior to moving to Florida in 1984, my husband, son, and I spent nineteen years in Southern California. This period of time provided us with many opportunities and experiences that were not available in the Philadelphia area. It was also a period of great personal growth for all of us, both individually and as a family unit.

However, we will never forget our roots. Though time has taken or replaced many of the people, places, and things we once knew, Southwest Philadelphia will always have a special place in our hearts, and the wonderful memories which we cherish will linger.

Here is an update on our families:

Mildred is a widow and makes her home in Georgia. She has two sons: Marshall Jr. and his wife, Marolyn, are retired and make their home in California. Philip, an award-winning, world-renowned Christian author, and his wife, Janet, make their home in Colorado.

Walter died in October 2008. His widow, Elsie, is retired and makes her home in New Jersey. They raised one son, Walter Jr., Ret. USN Lt. Cmdr. He has four children: Nathan, Matthew, Blake and Rachel and several grandchildren, and resides in New Jersey. Their daughter, Carol and her husband, Greg, and son, Michael, reside in Tennessee.

Violet is a widow, lives in Northeast Philadelphia, and has five children: Harry, a professor at the University of Nebraska, and his wife, Carol, have a son, Andrew; Dorothy and her husband, Larry (an Air Force officer), live in Colorado, and have five children and two grandchildren; Dolores and Dianne are both teachers and live in the Philadelphia area; and Deb and her husband, Michael, have two sons, David and Daniel, and live in Texas.

Jim served in the Army during the Korean Conflict, and received the Korean Service Medal W/I Bronze Star, National Defense Service Medal, and a Good Conduct Medal. He retired from ConRail (formerly the Pennsylvania Railroad) after thirty-four years of service, and passed away in February 2008.

Ruth and her husband, Charlie, live in Florida. They have one son, Brian Keith, a Certified Financial Planner ®. He and his wife, Michelle, a media specialist at a local elementary school, also live in Florida. They have one son, Andrew, a widower, who works with the Marines at the Pentagon in Washington, D.C., and one daughter, Kristy. She and her husband, Brandt, also live in Florida, where Kristy teaches school and Brandt is a journalist in the Admissions Department at Southeastern University, at Lakeland, Florida.

Bob, a widower, served in the Army during the mid-1950s, and was an engineer and a contractor. He lived in Florida prior to his death in December 2009. His daughter, Cynthia, died in June 1999; his son, Darrell, lives in Germany. Robin (the youngest daughter) is a widow. She and her two daughters, Bridgett and Brynn, live in Florida. Grace, his first wife, still lives in Florida. Mary, his second wife, died in December 2003.

Acknowledgements

My heartfelt thanks to my daughter-in-law, Michelle, for her very kind words of encouragement, and for lovingly sharing her technical expertise with me.

To Brandt Merritt, who willingly contributed to this memoir by sharing his expertise and for preparing the photographs which are included herein.

To Philip Yancey, my nephew, who has deeply honored me with his contribution by writing the Foreword. His unique writing style and very interesting, informative and insightful comments have truly enhanced this memoir.

To Stella Jackson, Director of Editing Services, Ann Staton, Book Production Coordinator, and their colleagues my thanks for patiently assisting and guiding me in getting this book published.

The valuable input that each of you gave toward this endeavor is sincerely appreciated.

A Tribute to Treasured Friendships

Life has blessed me with many wonderful friends, and I would be remiss if I did not acknowledge my close childhood friends who were a very important part of my past and with many of whom I am still in contact. The memories that we have shared over the years are very dear to me, and their friendships are deeply cherished: Jane (Holtz) Given, Kathy (Schoellkopf) Shields, Dolores (Walaitis) and Nick Norcini, Dolores (Benzing) and Bud Batty, Patti Yost, Ruth Trout, and Allan Jaffe.

Though separated by many miles through the years, and visits were and continue to be few and far between, my friendship with Jane Given has remained steadfast. It spans seven decades through which we have shared many, many experiences---some individually and others with our families and close friends. Some occasions were very happy and others were very sad, but we always knew we were there for each other with understanding; and to offer a listening ear and a caring word as the need arose. We have maintained very close contact throughout the years, and enjoy reminiscing about the past on the rare occasions when we have the opportunity to get together. Due to various reasons, I have resorted to using the keyboard and email for my communications. Jane, on the other hand, uses snail mail and her letters arrive still written in her beautiful penmanship. I am indeed grateful that when asked to contribute to this memoir, she graciously agreed.

* * * * *

Ruth's memoir, *Poor...but Very, Very Rich,* has taken me down memory lane, reliving my childhood with her. Ruth and I have been friends for seventy years. I met her when I moved to the street on which she and her family lived in Southwest Philadelphia in 1940, when I was nine years old.

We became close friends, sharing many of the experiences found in her book (school, church, and neighborhood). I was an only child and Ruth and her siblings became my extended family. Even though we are many miles away physically, we have been very close in spirit. Ruth has lived in California and

Florida while I have remained in the Philadelphia area all my life.

It is true, we were <u>POOR</u> but we didn't know it as we had our needs met daily; and also had the love of our earthly parents and our Heavenly Father.

A. Jane Given

List of Photographs

Ruth with friend Jane, circa 1940-1941
A Tribute to Treasured Friendships

Index

About the Author

Following retirement from a lengthy and successful career encompassing many facets of business, the author embarked on a new vocation by accepting employment as an instructional assistant/ILS at a high school in the Pasco County (Florida) school district. This experience provided the author with the opportunity to manage a computer-assisted instruction lab for drop-out prevention students, assisting them in developing reading, writing, and math skills.

The author led a number of workshops for students who had difficulty in passing the competency test required for graduation, as well as tutoring individual students and sharing test-preparation techniques.

She also organized and oversaw the management of the student-run school store, which sold school supplies and spirit items to meet student needs at a reduced cost. The profits were returned to the students by providing a number of scholarships to deserving graduating seniors.

In addition, Mrs. Lott served on the school advisory council for a number of years, chaired the attendance committee, organized and co-chaired a mentoring program, and served as a member of the literacy committee and also the CAPA board.

The author retired from the school district in June 2008. She and her husband, Charlie, have one son, a daughter-in-law, and two adult grandchildren. They make their home in Bayonet Point, Florida. The author is currently a member of the Pasco Writers group, and has also written *BK's Big Move Across the Country: From Philadelphia to L.A.*